TWO DISHES

LINDA HAYNES & DEVIN CONNELL

TWO DISHES

MOTHER AND DAUGHTER

TWO COOKS, TWO LIFESTYLES

TWO TAKES

McCLELLAND & STEWART

LIBRARY AND ARCHIVES CANADA CATALOGUING IN PUBLICATION

Haynes, Linda
    Two dishes : mother and daughter : two cooks, two lifestyles, two takes / Linda Haynes and Devin Connell.

  ISBN 978-0-7710-3816-7

    1. Cookery. I. Connell, Devin II. Title.

TX714.H39 2009   641.5   C2009-901417-3

We acknowledge the financial support of the Government of Canada through the Book Publishing Industry Development Program and that of the Government of Ontario through the Ontario Media Development Corporation's Ontario Book Initiative. We further acknowledge the support of the Canada Council for the Arts and the Ontario Arts Council for our publishing program.

ONTARIO ARTS COUNCIL
CONSEIL DES ARTS DE L'ONTARIO

Typeset in Filosofia by M&S, Toronto
Printed and bound in China

Photography by Douglas Bradshaw, except for the following: p. ii top left, top middle, bottom left, middle right; p. v; p. viii middle and bottom; p. ix middle and bottom; p. 19; p. 63; p. 75; p. 123; p. 145; p. 148.

Designed by Terri Nimmo

McClelland & Stewart Ltd.
75 Sherbourne Street
Toronto, Ontario
M5A 2P9
www.mcclelland.com

1   2   3   4   5   13   12   11   10   09

ALSO BY LINDA HAYNES

The ACE Bakery Cookbook

More from ACE Bakery

To Paulette Haynes (1913 — 2008)

*Beloved mom and nana
who inspired and taught both of us
in and out of the kitchen.*

CONTENTS

GROWING UP, MY FRIENDS WERE ALWAYS ANGLING for an invitation to dinner. The conversation was stimulating, and my parents treated my friends with interest and respect. But the real draw was my Belgian mother's cooking — elegant soups, roasts with red wine sauce, homemade French fries and mayonnaise, and thin-as-air crêpes.

Luckily my mom was happy to teach me all the secrets of her kitchen, but she never asked me to clean up — certainly an incentive to be creative.

When Martin and I married and had children, it was natural that a lot of family time centered around the dinner table.

Even as a child, Devin was always interested in the creative aspect of cooking, so I took a leaf out of my mother's book and showed her the basics, while never asking her to clean up. It was fascinating for me to watch Devin develop her own style. She brought back ideas and techniques from family travels, and when she moved away to go to university, she came up with inventive recipes that suited her time constraints, budget and tiny kitchen. Then she decided to spend a summer studying pastry making in Paris, and I knew the student no longer needed me as a teacher.

When she returned from Paris, Devin and I realized that our styles and cooking methods had diverged. While I like to plan a menu, Devin prefers to be spontaneous. I make up a basic grocery list and add on at the store. Devin lets the store's bounty inspire her. She will creatively substitute ingredients when they are not available at her local grocery store or farmers' market, while I don't think twice about traveling half an hour for one ingredient.

What we've both come to realize is that there are many ways to get to the desired conclusion, and so an idea was born — a recipe book that reflects the lifestyles and tastes of a mother and daughter who love to cook. And because we both love comfort food, we've included a special chapter — Good Eats for Bad Days — food that will cheer you up, any where, any time.

Even though Devin has now left home, we still cook together whenever we can. Our meals are an amalgamation of both our recipes. All the dishes in this book can be mixed and matched. Whether you're pulling together an elegant dinner for two or twenty, planning a make-ahead meal or looking for a last-minute dish or quick snack or brunch recipe, we hope you'll be able to find it in this book.

Linda

AFTER MOM WROTE HER FIRST TWO COOKBOOKS, she came to me with the idea of doing a cookbook together. At first I was a little concerned about working with my mother on a full-time basis (who wouldn't be), but it really seemed like a natural thing for us to do. A lot of our most fun, creative and exciting moments take place in the family kitchen. Shopping for food, cooking and eating at home or in restaurants are some of my favorite times with Mom.

At the same time, writing this cookbook with her was a challenge — I liken it to Napoleon's long winter march from Moscow to Paris. I figure just getting through this experience is a true testament to the unconditional nature of family love. As in most mother-daughter relationships, we have our share of fights, slammed doors and eye rolling, but we also share a lot of triumphs, excitement, encouragement and love.

When we were struggling through the final stages of this book, Mom said, "It's like childbirth. When it's all over and you see what you've got, it's worth it." I can't exactly relate (I don't have kids of my own), but I think it's an appropriate analogy.

I have learned almost everything I know about food from my mother: pairing flavors, timing, techniques and taste. During my years at university I missed Mom's cooking, and I learned to take her recipes and make substitutions if certain ingredients were unavailable or too expensive, or if my small kitchen didn't provide the space I needed to produce her culinary masterpieces.

Like most mothers and daughters, we have different ways of doing things — both in and out of the kitchen. We have learned that there is more than one way to get to where you want to be. It truly is all about options.

In this book we give you two takes on a similar theme. For example, Mom's tomato soup is slow cooked, with a few harder-to-find ingredients, while mine is quick, simple and budget-conscious. While the ingredients for my roast chicken with dried apricots and prosciutto can be picked up at any grocery store, Mom's seared duck breasts with dried cherries and shallots probably means a trip to a specialty butcher and greengrocer.

I think you get the idea. Both are worth trying, depending on your level of expertise, your time and your budget. It's all about making a recipe your own to suit your lifestyle, and you'll end up with a great result either way!

Devin

One of the nicest things someone can do for me is make me breakfast. It puts me in a good mood for the rest of the day.

LINDA

RISE AND SHINE

Although I usually just grab a boring low-fat yogurt when I'm halfway out the door, the weekend is the time for long and lazy breakfasts.

DEVIN

Linda

WILD BLUEBERRY, CINNAMON *and* OATMEAL SCONES

MAKES 8 LARGE SCONES

SCONES

2 cups unbleached all-purpose flour

½ cup granulated sugar

1 Tbsp baking powder

1 tsp kosher salt

½ tsp ground cinnamon

1 cup old-fashioned rolled oats

¾ cup unsalted butter, cold, cut in
  ½-inch cubes

½ cup 10% (half-and-half) cream

6 Tbsp crème fraîche (page 201)
  or sour cream

1 Tbsp lightly packed grated orange
  zest (about 1 medium),
  preferably organic

1 cup fresh or frozen (unthawed)
  blueberries

TOPPING

1 Tbsp 10% (half-and-half) cream

1½ tsp granulated sugar

When Devin was a child, blueberry pie was high on her list of favorites. Her younger brother, Luke, loved it, too — until the day he devoured half a pie and vowed never to eat blueberries again. This scone recipe was my attempt to convince Luke to give blueberries another try. Serve them with one of Devin's flavored honeys (page 33).

If you are using frozen berries, don't defrost them. If you do, they will turn the dough an unappetizing blue color.

And, yes, Luke likes them.

Preheat the oven to 375°F.

For the scones, sift the flour, sugar, baking powder, salt and cinnamon together into a large bowl. Whisk in the oats.

Add the butter and, using your fingers, combine it with the dry ingredients just until the mixture resembles coarse meal. Don't overblend.

In a separate bowl, whisk together the cream, crème fraîche and orange zest.

Add the liquid ingredients and blueberries to the dry ingredients. Stir until just combined, being careful not to overmix. (Cool hands are best.)

Gather the dough into a ball. Flatten it into a disk about 1¼ inches thick and 7 inches in diameter. Cut into 8 wedges. For the topping, brush the scones with cream and sprinkle with sugar.

Arrange the scones, about 1 inch apart, on a lightly greased or parchment-lined baking sheet. Bake for 25 to 30 minutes, or until golden brown. Transfer the scones to a rack for 15 to 20 minutes before serving.

Devin

SUMMER FRUIT MUFFINS
with PISTACHIO CRUNCH

These cakelike muffins are a delectable mix of colors, flavors and textures. They are perfect for breakfast or with afternoon tea. I freeze these little guys so I can have one whenever I want, which is really convenient with my erratic schedule. They can be stored in an airtight container at room temperature for up to two days or frozen for up to six weeks.

For the topping, combine the flour, sugar, pistachios and butter in a small bowl. Pinch the ingredients between your fingers until large, moist clumps form. Refrigerate the topping while you make the muffin batter.

Preheat the oven to 375°F. Line 12 large (½-cup) muffin cups with paper liners.

For the muffins, combine the flour, baking powder and salt in a bowl. I like to use a hand-held mixer on low for about 10 seconds (turning it any higher will cause a flour explosion).

In a large bowl, beat the butter and sugar with the mixer on high for 3 to 4 minutes, or until light and fluffy. Add the eggs and vanilla and beat on high for 2 minutes.

Add the flour mixture to the large bowl and beat on low until just combined, being sure to scrape down the sides of the bowl from time to time. Add the milk and beat on low just until combined. With a spatula, fold in the strawberries, nectarines and pistachios.

Spoon the batter into the muffin pan. Top the muffins with the reserved topping mixture, pressing it gently into the batter.

Bake for 22 to 25 minutes, or until the muffins are slightly golden and a cake tester inserted in the centers comes out clean. Remove the muffins from the pan and cool on a wire rack.

MAKES 12 LARGE MUFFINS

TOPPING

¼ cup unbleached all-purpose flour

2 Tbsp granulated sugar

½ cup chopped unsalted pistachios
   or pecans

3 Tbsp unsalted butter, cold, cut in
   ¼-inch cubes

MUFFINS

1¾ cups unbleached all-purpose flour

1½ tsp baking powder

½ tsp kosher salt

⅔ cup unsalted butter,
   at room temperature

1 cup granulated sugar

2 large eggs

2 tsp vanilla extract

½ cup whole milk

1 cup diced strawberries
   (about ¼-inch dice)

1 cup diced nectarines
   (about ¼-inch dice)

½ cup chopped unsalted pistachios
   or pecans

Linda

SUNDAY MORNING CRÊPES

4 large eggs

1 cup unbleached all-purpose flour

2 Tbsp granulated sugar

1¼ cups whole milk

3 Tbsp unsalted butter, approx.

When my brother, Phil, and I were kids, my mother would make crêpes most Sunday mornings. She sprinkled them with a little sugar and a tiny squeeze of lemon and rolled them up to eat, but I like to spread these with raspberry or apricot jam and fold them in quarters. You can also spoon on a thin layer of Nutella or Devin's chocolate butter (page 127) and top with slices of banana before folding.

KITCHEN HINT

CRÊPES 101

- Your first crêpe rarely looks good. Don't be discouraged. Think of it as a treat for the cook.
- Stove temperature is very important. If the temperature is too low, the crepes will be dry and leathery; if it is too hot, they will not be fully cooked in the middle. Medium-high heat often works best.
- Crêpes freeze well. Stack them on top of each other, wrap in plastic wrap, then in foil and freeze for up to a month. Thaw, wrapped, at room temperature. Remove the foil and plastic wrap and gently heat at 300°F until warm.

Whisk the eggs together in a large bowl. Slowly add the flour and then the sugar, whisking continuously. When the dry ingredients are incorporated, whisk in the milk in a slow but continuous steam. Let the batter sit for 10 minutes. It should have the consistency of very heavy cream and coat the back of a spoon. (Don't worry if there are small bits of flour in the batter. They will dissolve as the batter sits.)

Preheat the oven to 250°F.

Melt 1 tsp butter in an 8- or 9-inch crêpe pan or heavy-bottomed skillet over medium-high heat. (If you are making crêpes for the first time, you may want to use a nonstick pan.) As soon as the butter has stopped frothing, pour in ¼ cup batter. Quickly swirl the batter evenly over the bottom of the pan.

Cook the batter for about 1 minute. It should look slightly golden around the edges. Lift up a corner with a spatula or flipper. The bottom of the crêpe should be a warm golden color. Flip the crêpe and cook for about 30 to 45 seconds. The first side cooked is the presentation side. (The second side will look speckled and golden brown.)

Transfer the crêpe to an ovenproof dish and keep warm in the oven while you make the rest, adding a little butter to the pan as you need it (you will need less butter after the first few crêpes are made).

Devin

MAKE-AHEAD WHOLE WHEAT BANANA PANCAKES

What is so great about this recipe is that you can mix a big batch of the dry ingredients and then keep it for making pancakes any time you like without the hassle of busting out all of your bowls and measuring cups.

Despite being full of fiber and wholesome ingredients, these pancakes are incredibly light and fluffy. Just don't make them too big. Because of the different flours, they take longer to cook through than other pancakes, so if they're any bigger than 4 inches in diameter you'll end up with something that's burnt on the outside and raw in the middle.

This recipe can also be halved or doubled. (You can bet that each person will easily eat four.) Serve them with creamy plain yogurt and honey or, of course, maple syrup.

Add the dry pancake mix to a large bowl and make a well in the center.

In a separate bowl, mash the bananas and lightly beat in the eggs. Pour in the milk and combine.

Add the liquid ingredients to the flour mixture and stir just until combined. Allow the batter to sit for 5 minutes.

In a large skillet, heat 1 Tbsp butter over medium heat until it begins to bubble.

Pour in a scant ¼ cup batter for each pancake, gently smoothing the batter. Cook for about 4 minutes, or until bubbles begin to form in the center. Flip and continue to cook for 3 minutes, or until the pancakes are cooked through.

Repeat with the remaining butter and batter. (The pancakes can be kept warm, covered with foil, in a 200°F oven for up to 20 minutes.)

MAKES ABOUT 15 PANCAKES

1¾ cups dry pancake mix

2 bananas

2 large eggs

¾ cup whole milk

3 Tbsp unsalted butter, approx.

DRY PANCAKE MIX
Combine 1½ cups whole wheat flour, ½ cup unbleached all-purpose flour, ⅔ cup wheat germ, ⅔ cup wheat or oat bran, 2 Tbsp granulated sugar and 4 tsp baking powder.

Makes 3½ cups (enough for about 40 pancakes).

SERVES 4 TO 6

5 slices bacon, cut in ½-inch pieces

6 oz (175 g) fresh spinach
(about 1 bunch), trimmed

9 large eggs, used separately

3 green onions, white and light-green
parts only, finely chopped

½ tsp kosher salt

⅛ tsp freshly ground black pepper

2 Tbsp unsalted butter

⅓ cup grated Gruyère cheese
(about 1½ oz/45 g)

BACON, SPINACH *and*
GRUYÈRE FRITTATA SOUFFLÉ

If you're craving kitchen accolades, this is for you — easy to make, impressive to look at and absolutely delicious. The fact that spinach is a great source of vitamins A and C is a bonus.

Whipping the egg whites separately and folding them into the other ingredients makes this frittata lighter and airier than usual. It's a good brunch dish served with your favorite green salad and lots of buttered multigrain toast (page 30). Devin's Prosecco punch (page 35) adds a festive note on weekend mornings.

Cook the bacon in a large skillet until crisp. Drain on paper towels and reserve.

Bring a pot of water to a boil. Plunge the spinach into the water for about 45 seconds. Drain the spinach in a colander, pressing out as much water as possible. (You will be left with about ½ cup.) Pat dry and chop roughly.

Preheat the oven to 375°F.

Whisk 6 eggs in a bowl. Separate the 3 remaining eggs into whites and yolks. Whisk the 3 yolks into the whole eggs and put the whites in a separate bowl. Stir the bacon, spinach, green onions, salt and pepper into the whole eggs and egg yolks.

Beat the egg whites until very stiff peaks form. Gently fold into the egg mixture. Don't worry if small particles of egg white remain.

Melt the butter in a deep 8- or 9-inch ovenproof skillet over medium heat. Pour the eggs into the pan, making sure the bacon, spinach and onions are evenly distributed. Sprinkle the top with cheese and cook for 1½ minutes.

Place the skillet in the oven and bake for 16 or 18 minutes, or until the top has puffed and turns golden. Serve immediately.

VEGGIE VERSION

When I make this for the vegetarian members of the family, I sauté about 5 sliced small white mushrooms in a little butter and add them to the eggs instead of the bacon.

Devin

COCONUT FRENCH TOAST
with PINEAPPLE MAPLE SYRUP

I recently woke up on Sunday morning after a night out with my girlfriends and was craving French toast in the worst way. I never seem to have enough fresh milk on hand when I need it, but I did happen to have a can of coconut milk that I had bought ages ago for a curry recipe. I substituted the coconut milk for regular milk and ended up with an insanely flavorful and delicious dish.

Infusing maple syrup (make sure you splurge on the real stuff) with fresh pineapple creates the most spectacularly fragrant syrup you can imagine. (Next time I'm going to make a maple pineapple martini with the leftovers.) If piña colada came as a breakfast, this would be it!

Preheat the oven to 400°F.

For the syrup, heat the maple syrup, pineapple and nutmeg in a small saucepan over low heat. Leave the syrup to infuse over low heat while you prepare the French toast.

For the French toast, whisk together the eggs and coconut milk in a shallow dish.

Heat 1 Tbsp butter in a large skillet over medium-high heat until the butter is almost browned.

While the butter is heating, add half the bread to the coconut and egg mixture, letting it soak for 15 seconds per side. Lay the pieces of bread in the skillet and fry for 2 minutes on each side, or until you have a nice golden crust. Place the fried bread on a foil-lined baking sheet. Using the remaining 1 Tbsp butter, cook the second batch of French toast and place on the baking sheet.

Bake for 10 minutes.

Serve two overlapping slices per serving. Drizzle with the syrup and sprinkle with a little coconut if you wish.

SERVES 4 TO 6

PINEAPPLE MAPLE SYRUP

1 cup maple syrup

1 cup chopped fresh pineapple

Pinch of ground nutmeg

FRENCH TOAST

3 large eggs

1 14-oz (400 mL) can coconut
   milk, stirred

2 Tbsp butter, divided

4 to 6 slices day-old crusty white
   bread, about 1 inch thick,
   cut in half on the diagonal

Shaved fresh coconut, optional

· ·

KITCHEN HINT

COCONUT MILK: PULP FICTION
Coconut milk is an infusion of coconut meat and water (the clear liquid inside the coconut is called coconut juice or coconut water). It is a great substitute for dairy. I like to use the regular (not light) kind. Make sure you stir it up before using.

· ·

Linda

POACHED EGG CROSTINI *with* SMOKED SALMON, ASPARAGUS *and* DILL

SERVES 4

12 stalks asparagus, trimmed

4 slices dense white bread
(e.g., Calabrese), about ¾ inch thick

8 to 10 slices smoked salmon
(about 6 oz/175 g)

3 Tbsp white vinegar
(for poaching the eggs)

1 tsp kosher salt

4 large eggs

1½ Tbsp unsalted butter

2 Tbsp freshly squeezed lemon juice

1½ Tbsp lightly packed coarsely
chopped fresh dill

Sprigs of fresh dill, for garnish

Kosher salt and freshly ground
black pepper

I developed this recipe one spring as an alternative to Eggs Benedict. The salmon and dill remind me of Sweden, a country I lived in for a few years as a child.

Using fresh eggs will improve your chances of a perfect poach. The white of an egg thins out as it ages, which causes the sometimes cloudy mess that egg whites can leave behind in the water.

The asparagus and eggs (see hint) can be prepared ahead of time, so all you have to do to get this delicious dish to the table is grill or toast the bread and melt the butter. Bring the asparagus to room temperature before continuing with the recipe or, if you want warm asparagus, plunge the stalks into boiling water for 30 seconds and pat dry just before assembling the dish.

For bigger appetites, poach more eggs and place two eggs on each crostini.

Bring a large skillet of water to a boil. Plunge the asparagus into the water and cook for 2 to 4 minutes (depending on the thickness of the stalks), or until it is bright green and still slightly crisp. Submerge in cold water to stop the cooking process. Drain and pat dry.

Grill or toast the bread. Place on individual plates and drape with smoked salmon.

To poach perfect eggs you need a wide, deep saucepan filled three-quarters full with water and the vinegar. Bring it to a boil and add the salt. Reduce the water to a simmer.

Break an egg into a cup or ramekin and gently slide it out of the cup into the simmering water. Once you have added all the eggs, scoop off the foam that rises to the top of the water. Poach the eggs for 3 minutes.

Remove the eggs from the water with a slotted spoon. Rest the spoon for a moment on a piece of bread or sheet of paper towel to remove excess moisture. Gently lay the eggs on top of the smoked salmon. Top each egg with 3 stalks of asparagus.

Melt the butter in a small saucepan. Stir in the lemon juice and chopped dill and pour evenly over the eggs. Top with a sprig of dill, sprinkle with salt and pepper and serve immediately.

KITCHEN HINT

GETTING INTO HOT WATER:
MAKE-AHEAD POACHED EGGS

If you want to prepare your eggs ahead of time, poach the eggs and place them in a bowl of cold water. Refrigerate them in the water for up to 24 hours. Just before serving, lift out the eggs and plunge them into simmering water for 1½ minutes to warm up.

Devin

SPICY SALSA

½ green bell pepper, seeded and diced

1 cup seeded and diced tomato

2 tsp finely chopped jalapeño

1 Tbsp lightly packed finely chopped
    fresh cilantro

1 Tbsp freshly squeezed lime juice

½ tsp kosher salt

¼ tsp freshly ground black pepper

EGGS

3 Tbsp white wine vinegar
    (for poaching the eggs)

1 tsp kosher salt

4 large eggs

4 small Boston or iceberg leaves

POACHED HUEVOS IN
LETTUCE LEAVES *with* SPICY SALSA

Poaching eggs can a bit of a challenge, but my mom's method is painless. What I like about this breakfast is that it's super healthy and full of flavor. If you've had an indulgent dinner the night before, this easy recipe will help get you back on track (though Mom would never accept eating eggs without toast!).

For the salsa, in a bowl, combine the green pepper, tomato, jalapeño, cilantro, lime juice, salt and pepper. Set aside to marinate while you poach the eggs.

To poach the eggs, fill a wide, deep saucepan three-quarters full with water and add the vinegar. Bring it to a boil and add the salt. Reduce the water to a simmer.

Break an egg into a cup or ramekin and gently slide the egg into the simmering water. Repeat with the remaining eggs and scoop off the foam that rises to the surface of the water. Poach the eggs for 3 minutes.

Remove the eggs from the water with a slotted spoon. Rest the spoon on a piece of bread or paper towel to remove excess moisture.

Place two lettuce "cups" on each plate. Gently put a poached egg in each cup. Spoon the salsa around the lettuce and eggs. Serve immediately.

SERVES 4

8 paper-thin slices pancetta

2 Tbsp extra-virgin olive oil, divided

½ red bell pepper, seeded and
cut in strips

½ yellow bell pepper, seeded and
cut in strips

½ green bell pepper, seeded and
cut in strips

1 small cooking onion, thinly sliced

2 cloves garlic, finely chopped

2 28-oz (796 mL) cans plum tomatoes,
drained and roughly chopped

6 fresh basil leaves, shredded

4 large eggs

4 slices sourdough or other dense
white bread, about ½ inch thick

¼ cup lightly packed coarsely chopped
flat-leaf parsley

Kosher salt and freshly ground
black pepper to taste

SKILLET-BAKED EGGS *with* CRISPY PANCETTA ON TOMATO PEPPER RAGOUT

Devin and I both love one-dish breakfasts. This recipe contains pancetta, fried eggs and tomato sauce, while Devin whisks her eggs into cream and bakes it with bacon and English muffins (page 28). You can prepare the ragout up to two days ahead. (It also freezes beautifully.) Add more eggs for bigger appetites. Luke, a cheese fanatic, always sprinkles a few spoonfuls of grated Parmesan or crumbled goat cheese on top at the end.

Fry the pancetta in a skillet over high heat until crisp, about 30 seconds per side. Drain on paper towels and set aside.

Add 1 Tbsp oil and the peppers to a large cold skillet. Heat over medium-high and sauté the peppers until soft, about 10 minutes. Remove the peppers from the pan and set aside. Reduce the heat to medium.

Add the remaining 1 Tbsp oil to the same skillet. Add the onion and garlic. Sauté for 7 to 8 minutes, or until the onions are soft and pale golden.

Increase the heat to medium-high. Add the tomatoes and cook for 5 minutes. Throw in the reserved peppers and basil and simmer for 5 minutes.

With a large spoon, create four indentations in the tomato-pepper mixture. Drop an egg into each hollow. Cover and cook for about 4 minutes, or until the whites are cooked.

While the eggs are cooking, grill or toast the bread. Place a slice in each of 4 shallow bowls. Carefully top each slice with ragout and an egg. Sprinkle with parsley, salt and pepper. Arrange the pancetta slices decoratively over the top. For a more casual presentation, take the skillet to the table and serve directly into shallow bowls.

KITCHEN HINTS

BELL PEPPERS

All peppers start out green, but as they ripen their sugar content increases, making them sweeter as they turn red, orange and yellow. Full of vitamin C, they also contain beta carotene, thought to protect against heart disease and some cancers.

To seed peppers quickly, try the chef's trick of standing them up on a cutting board and cutting away four sides, leaving the core and seeds behind.

PANCETTA

Pancetta (pronounced "pan-CHEH-tah") is pork belly that has been salted, cured or soaked in brine, sometimes spiced and dried for up to three months. It comes in two forms: straight with the fat on one side or rolled in a salami shape. Unlike bacon, it is rarely smoked.

Devin

6 large eggs

2 cups 35% (whipping) cream

1 cup whole milk

2 Tbsp Dijon mustard

2 Tbsp lightly packed finely chopped
    fresh chives

1½ tsp kosher salt

½ tsp freshly ground black pepper

1 lb (500 g) bacon,
    cut in ½-inch pieces

10 English muffins,
    cut in half horizontally

1⅓ cups hollandaise sauce

EGGS BENEDICT BREAD PUDDING
with MOM'S FOOLPROOF HOLLANDAISE

If you love Eggs Benedict, just imagine a huge, golden, crispy dish of Eggs Benedict that you can feed to a crowd. No worrying about poaching eggs or toasting the English muffins at the last minute. Instead, an intense egg custard gives this dish its silky, rich flavor. The hollandaise is also super simple and you can make it while the bread pudding is settling.

Preheat the oven to 350°F.

In a large jug or measuring cup, whisk together the eggs, cream, milk, mustard, chives, salt and pepper.

In a large skillet, sauté the bacon until crisp. Drain on paper towels and set aside.

Generously butter a 13- by 9-inch baking dish. Line the bottom of the dish with a layer of halved muffins, cut side up and overlapping slightly.

Scatter the bacon over the muffins and then pour half the egg mixture over top, allowing the muffins to soak up the liquid.

Arrange the remaining muffins cut side down over the eggs. (You might have to cut some of the muffin halves again to fill any large gaps.)

Pour the remaining milk mixture over the top and press the muffins down to help them absorb the liquid. Let rest for 10 to 20 minutes.

Place the baking dish on a baking sheet and bake for about 65 minutes, or until the top is golden brown and the liquid is set.

Let rest for 10 minutes before serving. Serve using a large spoon or spatula, trying to give each person a full muffin. Drizzle with hollandaise.

MOM'S FOOLPROOF HOLLANDAISE

In a small saucepan, combine 4 lightly beaten egg yolks, 4 tsp freshly squeezed lemon juice, ½ tsp kosher salt and 1 Tbsp 35% (whipping) cream. Add a 1-cup block of very cold butter and refrigerate for 10 minutes (this will help to prevent the sauce from separating).

Place the saucepan over low heat and continuously swirl the butter with a spoon as it melts into the eggs and cream. Once the butter has melted, continue to stir for a total of about 12 minutes. The sauce will thicken to a consistency somewhere between heavy cream and a thin mayonnaise. Serve immediately.

Makes 1⅓ cups.

Linda

MULTIGRAIN BREAD

MAKES 2 LOAVES

STARTER

½ tsp traditional dry yeast

2 tsp lukewarm water

½ cup + ⅓ cup cool water

9 oz (255 g) unbleached
   hard white flour

1 tsp kosher salt

BREAD DOUGH

.7 oz (20 g) bulgur

.7 oz (20 g) rye flakes

.7 oz (20 g) untoasted
   buckwheat groats

.7 oz (20 g) oat flour

.7 oz (20 g) sunflower seeds

.7 oz (20 g) flax seeds

.7 oz (20 g) old-fashioned rolled oats

.7 oz (20 g) rye flour

½ cup + 1 tsp lukewarm water

½ tsp traditional dry yeast

2 tsp lukewarm water

1 cup cool water

9¾ oz (275 g) unbleached
   hard white flour

2 Tbsp liquid honey

3¼ oz (90 g) starter

2 tsp kosher salt

3 Tbsp vegetable oil

This is a home version of ACE Bakery's bestselling multigrain bread. Because of the touch of honey and the good oils in the grains and seeds, it stays fresh longer than bread made exclusively with flour.

Don't be put off by the length of the recipe. In reality you will spend ten minutes making the starter and another thirty to forty minutes, in dribs and drabs, mixing and shaping the dough. I find that the job becomes much easier if I assemble and measure all my ingredients before I start. You'll notice that the ingredients are weighed, except for small amounts that I felt were too tiny to register on a home scale. I have had only bad experiences making bread using volume measurements.

For the starter, stir the yeast into the warm water (75° to 90°F/24° to 32°C) in a small bowl. The yeast should take on a creamy-looking consistency within a few minutes.

Pour the yeast into the bowl of a standing mixer fitted with a dough hook. Add the cool water (65°F/18°C), flour and salt. Mix on slow (speed 1) for 1 minute. Scrape down the sides of the bowl with a plastic spatula as needed. Increase the speed to fast (speed 3) and mix for 3 minutes.

Place the starter in a lightly oiled medium bowl and cover with plastic wrap. Refrigerate for 12 to 13 hours OR leave at room temperature (70° to 74°F/21 to 23°C) in a draft-free area for 2 hours and then refrigerate for 4 hours. (The starter will then need to sit at room temperature for 1½ hours before using.)

To make the bread, combine the bulgur, rye flakes, buckwheat, oat flour, sunflower seeds, flax seeds, rolled oats, rye flour and lukewarm water in a bowl. Let stand for 2 hours.

Meanwhile, remove the starter from the fridge and bring it to 55° to 60°F (12° to 15°C). This should take 1 to 1½ hours.

Put the yeast and 2 tsp warm water in the bowl of a standing mixer fitted with a dough hook. Whisk it together to dissolve the yeast. Add 1 cup cool water, white flour, honey, starter, salt and oil to the bowl and mix for 1 minute on stir speed and then 7 minutes on slow (speed 2). Scrape down the sides of the bowl with a spatula. Cover the bowl loosely with a kitchen towel and autolyse (rest) the dough for 15 minutes.

Add the soaked grains and flours to the dough and mix for 1 minute on stir and then 2 minutes on fast (speed 3). The dough should be at room temperature.

Lightly oil a large bowl. Scrape the dough, which will be sticky, onto a floured surface. Gently pull and shape it into a loose ball and place it in the oiled bowl, turning it around so it is covered in a thin film of oil. Cover loosely with plastic wrap or a tea towel and let rest in a draft-free area at room temperature for 1¼ hours.

Lightly oil two 7- by 3- by 2-inch loaf pans, preferably nonstick. Divide the dough in half. Gently pat each piece of dough into an 8- by 5½-inch rectangle. Use the palms of your hands to roll the dough lengthwise into a long jellyroll and pat into a shape that will fit your pan. Gently press the seams together. Put the dough in the pans seam side down. Again, cover loosely with a kitchen towel or lightly oiled plastic wrap. Let rise for about 1¼ hours. Preheat the oven to 375°F.

Press a finger into the dough. If the indentation remains, the bread is ready to be baked. If the dough springs back, rest for another 10 to 15 minutes and check again.

Spray the top of the loaves with water and immediately place on the middle rack of the oven. Bake for 45 minutes.

Remove the bread from the pans. It should be golden brown and produce a hollow sound when you tap the bottom. Bake for another 3 to 5 minutes if necessary. Cool on racks for at least 1 hour.

KITCHEN HINT

BREAD-MAKING 101

- Whenever possible, use a kitchen scale to measure ingredients, as weight measurements will be more accurate than volume measurements. Different flours, even different salts, will weigh the same but their volumes will be different.
- Begin by making a schedule of when each step should take place. Leave the schedule beside your bowl or pan.
- You will need a standing mixer with a dough hook, a low-temperature thermometer, a spray bottle, an oven thermometer, and patience.
- Always cover your dough after each step to prevent it from forming a dry crust that will inhibit rising.
- The optimum temperature for your finished dough before it goes into the oven should be 74° to 75°F (23° to 24°C). Dough will rise faster in a warmer kitchen.
- Store bread in a paper or cloth bag at room temperature. A plastic bag will soften the crust, and refrigeration draws out the moisture.

Devin

STEEPED HONEYS

There isn't a chance you will find me baking bread from scratch, but I will spend a little time making interesting things to put on it. This is one of the easiest ways to add flavor to your cooking. I use honey everywhere — on my toast in the morning, in meat marinades, salad dressings and teas (try using the lemongrass honey in the broccoli recipe on page 161). By spending just half an hour infusing bland white honey with gorgeous herbs and spices, you will have a wonderful condiment that will last for weeks.

Heat the honey in a small saucepan over medium heat. Add your choice of flavoring and heat for about 7 minutes, or until the honey begins to foam. Remove from the heat and let cool for 5 minutes.

With tongs, carefully remove the flavorings from the honey and place them in the original honey jar. Pour the warm honey back into the jar. I keep the honey at room temperature for a couple of weeks, though the flavor becomes slightly stronger the longer the herbs are left in the honey. After that I usually remove the herbs and keep the honey in fridge.

CINNAMON LEMONGRASS HONEY
1 18-oz (500 g) jar (glass) liquid honey

3 2-inch cinnamon sticks

2 2-inch pieces lemongrass

THYME HONEY
1 18-oz (500 g) jar (glass) liquid honey

10 sprigs fresh thyme

SAGE HONEY
1 18-oz (500 g) jar (glass) liquid honey

15 fresh sage leaves

LEMONGRASS MINT INFUSION
A cup or two of this sweet/tart infusion is the perfect digestif. Lemongrass is used in South America and Africa to soothe headaches and fevers and aid digestion. Mint, rich in vitamin A, also has settling properties and quells nausea.

Lemongrass stalks can be frozen, tightly wrapped, for up to month.

Rinse and gently smash a 2-inch piece of lemongrass (including the bulb), then cut it into thin slices. Crumple ½ cup fresh mint leaves in your hand and place them in a tea pot with the lemongrass.

Add 6 cups boiling water and steep for 10 minutes before pouring.

Makes about 6 cups.

Linda

TRUE MOROCCAN MINT TEA

SERVES 2

2 tsp loose green gunpowder tea

3 cups boiling water

2 cups packed fresh mint leaves

2 Tbsp granulated sugar

Mint tea, usually served in Morocco from a metal tea pot, is believed to engage all the senses: touch, taste, smell, sight and even sound, as the tea is traditionally poured from a great height into small tea glasses, creating a delicate splashing sound and a slight froth. The tea is poured back and forth between the pot and glasses several times as both a ritual and to aid in the brewing process.

The only thing that is not authentic about this recipe is that I use much less sugar than you would use in Morocco.

Heat the tea pot with hot water. Pour the water out and add the gunpowder tea to the pot. Pour in the boiling water and let sit for 2 minutes.

Pour 2 cups tea into a tea glass or cup and return to the tea pot. Add the mint and sugar to the tea and let sit for another minute. Pour 2 cups tea into a glass or cup and again return to the pot.

Your tea is now ready to drink.

Devin

HONEYBEE PROSECCO PUNCH
(photo page 25)

Mom's mint tea may suit all you teatotalers, but I happen to have a mild fondness for a good cocktail at brunch. After a late one, this punch acts as a morning pick-me-up. Antioxidants + vitamin C + Prosecco = Number One Rescue Remedy. And don't relegate this lovely tipple to brunch. It's absolutely heavenly at any time of day.

I truly think I've come across the best rim detail for any mixed drink. For those of you who shiver at the rim of salt on a Margarita, here is the answer. (When I'm at my parents' house I use Cognac in this, but it's pretty good with regular brandy, too!)

In a large glass pitcher, combine the Prosecco, Cognac, orange juice, pomegranate juice and ice. Stir gently.

Place the honey in a shallow dish. Lightly dip the rim of each glass (a wine or highball glass works best) into the honey to coat. Fill each glass with punch. Garnish with a few rosemary leaves.

SERVES 6

3 cups Prosecco or
   other sparkling white wine
   (1 bottle)

¼ cup Cognac

1 cup freshly squeezed orange juice
   (about 3 medium)

½ cup pomegranate juice

2 cups ice cubes

¼ cup liquid honey

1 sprig fresh rosemary

Serving little bites with drinks always signals that there will be a leisurely night ahead. Bowls of nuts are predictable. Try to be a little more adventurous.

LINDA

NIBBLES, SNACKS AND MEZZE

Drinks and nibbles are a great and inexpensive way to entertain. Sometimes the best dinners are two or three small plates of food that you can graze over all evening with a glass of wine.

DEVIN

Crunchy Spiced Chickpeas	38	Chili and Honey Popcorn	39
Indian Vegetable Pakora with Garam Masala Dip	40	Blistered Eggplant, Goat Cheese and Basil Dip	43
Melted Gruyère Croquettes	44	Crispy Potato Crostini with Taleggio, Apple and Prosciutto	47
Rosemary Farinata	48	Baked Pear, Cheese and Rosemary Crostini	49
Radish Chive Fromage Frais	50	Baked Lemony Feta Cheese with Thyme, Rosemary and Black Pepper	51
Sesame Tuna Bites with Cilantro Mint Chutney	52	Baby Lamb Meatballs with Pomegranate Yogurt Dip	55

Linda

CRUNCHY SPICED CHICKPEAS

19-oz (540 mL) can chickpeas,
rinsed and drained

2 tsp lightly packed minced
fresh thyme, divided

2 tsp lightly packed minced
fresh rosemary, divided

2 tsp lightly packed minced
fresh sage, divided

½ tsp kosher salt

¼ tsp freshly ground black pepper

2 Tbsp extra-virgin olive oil

1 tsp lightly packed grated lemon zest,
preferably organic

These are my Italian version of the crunchy Japanese wasabi peas. Perfect for serving with cocktails, they are salty, lemony and loaded with fresh herbs.

The chickpeas can be stored in an airtight container for up to a week.

Preheat the oven to 400°F.

Spread the chickpeas on a baking sheet. Sprinkle with 1 tsp thyme, 1 tsp rosemary, 1 tsp sage, the salt, pepper and oil and toss to combine.

Bake for 45 minutes, stirring every 10 minutes. The chickpeas should be crunchy all the way through.

Toss the warm chickpeas with the remaining thyme, rosemary, sage and the lemon zest. Serve warm or at room temperature.

Devin

CHILI *and* HONEY POPCORN

MAKES 6 CUPS

Back in university, I learned how to make pretty much anything using a microwave and an electric kettle. Turning a regular bag of microwave popcorn into a sophisticated nibble was a simple task, and I felt like I was instantly elevated out of the world of dorm food.

   This recipe is as simple as it sounds and takes less than 10 minutes to make (try the variation, too). Served with drinks or as a more interesting movie-night treat, you will be hard pressed not to eat the whole bowl.

In a small saucepan, melt the butter over low heat. Stir in the honey, salt and chili powder.

In a large bowl, toss the warm popcorn with the melted butter mixture to coat evenly.

3 Tbsp unsalted butter

3 Tbsp liquid honey

½ tsp sea salt

½ tsp chili powder

3-oz (85 g) bag popped popcorn
   (natural flavor, unbuttered)

BLACK PEPPER, BASIL AND PARMESAN POPCORN
In a large bowl, toss a 3-oz (85 g) bag popped popcorn (natural flavor, unbuttered) with 3 Tbsp extra-virgin olive oil. Sprinkle on 1 cup lightly packed finely grated Parmesan cheese (about 3 oz/90 g), 1 Tbsp lightly packed finely chopped fresh basil, ½ tsp kosher salt and ½ tsp freshly ground black pepper. Toss to combine.

Linda

INDIAN VEGETABLE PAKORA
with GARAM MASALA DIP

VEGETABLE PAKORA

¾ cup plus 2 generous Tbsp
   chickpea flour

1½ tsp garam masala

¾ tsp baking powder

½ tsp kosher salt

¼ tsp Indian red chili powder,
   or ⅛ tsp cayenne pepper

1 cup cold water

1 lb (500 g) any combination of
   red bell peppers, cauliflower,
   broccoli, spinach, carrot or
   red onion

Vegetable oil for frying

GARAM MASALA DIP

⅔ cup whole milk yogurt

1½ tsp ketchup

1 tsp garam masala

¼ tsp Indian red chili powder,
   or ⅛ tsp cayenne pepper

The mother of my friend Nalini taught me how to make this many years ago. It's a very easy northern India recipe that is a perfect appetizer or first course when you are having a casual dinner with friends. I like to invite my guests into the kitchen, pour them a glass of wine or beer and serve the pakora at the counter, but if you prefer to keep your kitchen to yourself, the pieces can be held in a warm oven for up to a half hour.

Chickpea flour, garam masala and Indian red chili powder can be found in the imported food section of most grocery stores. They should keep in your pantry, well wrapped, for six months.

For the pakora, combine the flour, garam masala, baking powder, salt and chili powder in a large bowl. Whisk in the cold water in a steady stream. Let sit for 30 minutes. The mixture should have the consistency of pancake batter. If it becomes too thick, whisk in a little more cold water.

Cut the peppers into 1-inch slices and the cauliflower and broccoli into small to medium florets. Peel the carrot and cut into ½-inch slices on the diagonal. Remove the stems from the spinach. Slice the onion into 1-inch wedges and separate into individual layers.

For the dip, combine the yogurt, ketchup, garam masala and chili powder in a small bowl.

Pour 2 inches of oil into a large saucepan. Heat the oil to 350°F/180°C (page 45).

Dip the vegetables in the batter. Tap them gently against the side of the bowl to remove excess batter. Plunge the vegetables one at a time into the hot oil (so they don't stick to each other) and cook in batches until the batter is a pale golden color, about 1 minute. Drain on paper towels and eat immediately with the dipping sauce, or place in a preheated 350°F oven until all the vegetables are cooked.

Devin

BLISTERED EGGPLANT, GOAT CHEESE *and* BASIL DIP

I love Mom's Indian pakora, but in my loft apartment there's nowhere to hide dirty pots and pans. I can make this dip in advance, which gives me time to clean up before my friends arrive. Charring the eggplant in a super-hot oven gives this dip a wonderful smoky flavor. It's phenomenal as an accompaniment for fresh veggies or as a spread on sandwiches (if you have any left over!). It should keep in the fridge for up to three days, and the flavor intensifies as it sits.

I like to serve this with crudités or crostini.

Preheat the oven to 450°F.

Cut the eggplants into large wedges and place skin side down on a baking sheet. Drizzle evenly with the oil and sprinkle with the salt and pepper. Bake for 15 minutes.

Rub the garlic clove with a little oil and place on the baking sheet with the eggplant. Return the eggplant and garlic to the oven and bake for another 15 minutes, or until the eggplant is slightly charred and the garlic is soft and caramelized (the total cooking time for the eggplant will be about 30 minutes).

While the eggplant is in the oven, mix together the goat cheese, lemon juice and basil in a bowl.

Allow the eggplant to cool slightly before scraping the flesh from the skin with a spoon.

Mash the cooked eggplant and softened garlic clove into the cheese mixture. Serve warm or at room temperature.

MAKES ABOUT 2 CUPS

2 Italian eggplants
(about 1½ lbs/750 g total)

2 Tbsp extra-virgin olive oil

1¼ tsp kosher salt

¼ tsp freshly ground black pepper

1 clove garlic, peeled

5 oz (150 g) goat cheese

2 Tbsp freshly squeezed lemon juice
(about ½ medium)

3 Tbsp lightly packed finely
chopped fresh basil

Linda

MELTED GRUYÈRE CROQUETTES

MAKES ABOUT 30 TO 35
CROQUETTES

FILLING

2 cups whole milk

½ cup unsalted butter

½ cup unbleached all-purpose flour

¾ tsp kosher salt

¼ tsp freshly ground white pepper

¼ tsp ground nutmeg

3 large eggs

3½ cups grated Gruyère cheese
(about 8 oz/250 g)

COATING

⅓ cup unbleached all-purpose flour

3 large egg whites

2 cups fine fresh breadcrumbs

Vegetable oil for frying

My mother used to make these spectacular warm molten croquettes when she entertained friends in Belgium during World War II. Because food was rationed, entertaining often took place around drinks and nibbles instead of at dinner.

The filling can be made up to 48 hours ahead and the small pieces of batter can be breaded 12 hours before your friends turn up. The finished product will keep in a warm oven for about a half hour. You could also serve two or three with a small green salad as an appetizer or as a cheese course.

Use good-quality Gruyère and panko or homemade breadcrumbs (page 105).

For the filling, bring the milk to a simmer in a small saucepan. Set aside.

Melt the butter in a large saucepan over medium heat. Add the flour a third at a time, stirring after each addition. Continue to stir and cook for about 45 seconds, or until the mixture is thoroughly combined and pale golden.

Keep stirring and gradually pour in the warm milk. Simmer for 2 minutes. Add the salt, pepper and nutmeg and remove from the heat.

Whisk the eggs in a bowl. Quickly, in three parts, stir the eggs into the warm mixture. Add the cheese and stir until all the cheese has melted.

Spoon the mixture into a 13- by 9-inch baking dish. The mixture should be about 2 inches deep. Cover and refrigerate until cool.

For the coating, put the flour in a shallow dish. Lightly whisk the egg whites in another shallow dish until just combined. Place the breadcrumbs in a third dish.

Using a tablespoon, scoop small balls of the cheese mixture (the size of a chocolate truffle) and place on a lightly greased baking sheet. (This is a messy job; it helps to moisten your hands with a touch of oil when forming the croquettes.)

One by one, lightly coat the croquettes with flour, dip in the egg white (covering all sides), and then roll in the breadcrumbs. Don't worry if the croquettes are slightly different in size and shape. Cover and refrigerate. Remove from the refrigerator 30 minutes before frying.

Preheat the oven to 275°F.

In a large, deep saucepan, heat ½-inch oil to 350°F (180°C).

Using a slotted spoon or Chinese sieve, gently lower 4 or 5 croquettes into the oil. Fry for 30 to 45 seconds on each side, or until golden brown. Place on a paper towel-lined baking sheet and place in the oven to keep warm. They will hold for about 30 minutes, though they will be a little more crispy if eaten immediately.

· ·

KITCHEN HINT

FRYING 101

If you don't have a deep-fry thermometer, here are two quick ways to test the temperature of the oil.

Drop a little batter into the hot oil. If the batter drops partway into the oil, then quickly rises, it's time to get cooking. If the batter falls to the bottom of the pot before rising, the oil is a bit too hot.

Or, drop a cube of bread into the hot oil. If it turns golden brown in 35 to 40 seconds, your oil is about 350°F (180°C) and ready for deep-frying.

· ·

Devin

CRISPY POTATO CROSTINI *with* TALEGGIO, APPLE *and* PROSCIUTTO

I love Mom's cheese croquettes, but I find the deep-frying business a little daunting. These are elegant bite-sized morsels for when you want to serve something other than your standard cheese and crackers. This recipe satisfies my craving for melted cheese, but only requires the use of my oven to get it. I also like the twist of using a slice of potato as the base instead of the usual slice of bread (try to use a potato with an even width, so the slices are more or less the same size).

Preheat the oven to 425°F. Place a baking sheet in the oven while it preheats. This will help crisp the potato slices.

Wash the potato but do not peel. Cut it into slices about ⅛ inch thick (you should have about 20 slices).

Coat the hot baking sheet with the oil and place the potato slices on the baking sheet in a single layer. Bake for 8 minutes on the bottom rack. Flip the potatoes and bake for 7 to 12 minutes longer, or until they are golden, cooked through and slightly crisp.

While the potato slices are in the oven, cut the cheese into 20 slices about ¼ inch thick and 2 inches long (long enough to cover the potato slices without hanging over the edges).

Tear each prosciutto slice into 4 pieces. Core the apple, cut it into paper-thin slices and sprinkle with lemon juice to prevent them from turning brown.

Place a piece of cheese on each potato slice. Return to the oven for 1 to 2 minutes, or until the cheese has just melted. Top each potato with a couple of apple slices and a twisted piece of prosciutto. Finish with a sprinkle of salt and pepper. Serve warm.

MAKES 20 CROSTINI

1 large baking potato (about 10 oz/ 300 g)

2 Tbsp extra-virgin olive oil

5 oz (150 g) Taleggio cheese, rind removed

5 thin slices prosciutto

1 Golden Delicious apple

2 Tbsp freshly squeezed lemon juice

½ tsp kosher salt

¼ tsp freshly ground black pepper

KITCHEN HINT

TALEGGIO
Taleggio is a wonderful soft cow's milk cheese from the Taleggio Valley near Bergamo in Lombardy. It melts amazingly, but if it is hard to find or a bit pricy, use Brie instead.

To cut the cheese thinly, stick it in the freezer for about 20 minutes before slicing.

Linda

1 cup plus 2 Tbsp chickpea flour

1½ cups cold water

¼ cup extra-virgin olive oil

1 Tbsp lightly packed coarsely
   chopped fresh rosemary

½ tsp kosher salt

¼ tsp freshly ground black pepper

Vegetable oil for frying

Large flaked sea salt

ROSEMARY FARINATA
(photo page 54)

Farinata, basically a thick, savory crêpe that is cut in wedges, is
called *calda, calda* (hot, hot) by the Tuscans. We serve it with
drinks before casual dinners. If you like, you can throw a handful of pitted black olives into the batter before it goes into the pan.

   Salmon (page 130) or roast chicken (page 146) would be a good
main to follow this. For dessert, I'd opt for Devin's mini apple tarts
(page 205).

   Chickpea flour can be found in health food stores or in the imported food section in most grocery stores.

In a large bowl, whisk together the flour and cold water. Set
aside for 30 minutes.

Preheat the oven to 500°F.

Whisk the oil, rosemary, salt and pepper into the batter. It
should have the consistency of heavy cream.

Heat a 10-inch cast-iron skillet over high heat until it is very hot.
If your pan is smaller, don't use all the batter. Generously coat
the bottom of the pan with oil. Add the batter (it should be
no more than ¼ inch thick) and cook for 1 to 2 minutes, or until
the batter starts to set around the edges and small bubbles
appear on the surface.

Transfer the frying pan to the oven and bake for about 20 minutes,
or until the batter is cooked through and the top is a motley
golden brown. Place under the broiler for 2 to 3 minutes if
you prefer a darker top. Slide onto a serving plate and sprinkle
with sea salt. Let sit for a few minutes before cutting into
thin wedges.

Devin

BAKED PEAR, CHEESE
and ROSEMARY CROSTINI

This is a great vegetarian hors d'oeuvre. Pear and rosemary (a herb Mom and I both love) make for a fantastic taste combination.

The best part is that you can make the topping well in advance (even a day before) and spread it on the bread a couple of hours before you plan to serve it. Just pop it in the oven at the last minute.

Substitute cream cheese for the goat cheese in a pinch.

Preheat the oven to 400°F.

Combine the goat cheese, Parmesan, chopped rosemary, salt and pepper in a bowl.

Spread the cheese mixture evenly over the baguette slices and place on a foil-lined baking sheet.

Bake for 10 minutes. Top each piece with some diced pear, coarsely ground pepper and a couple of rosemary leaves and serve hot.

5 oz (150 g) goat cheese, at room temperature

1 cup lightly packed finely grated Parmesan cheese (about 3 oz/90 g)

½ tsp lightly packed chopped fresh rosemary

½ tsp kosher salt

⅛ tsp freshly ground black pepper

20 slices baguette, about ½ inch thick

¾ cup finely diced unpeeled Bosc pear (about 1 small)

Coarsely ground black pepper

2 fresh rosemary sprigs

Linda

RADISH CHIVE FROMAGE FRAIS

FROMAGE FRAIS

6 cups whole milk

3 Tbsp freshly squeezed lemon juice

½ tsp kosher salt

SEASONINGS

¼ cup finely chopped radish

2 Tbsp lightly packed finely
   chopped chives

⅛ tsp freshly ground black pepper

Sea salt to taste

**BLACK PEPPER
DILL FROMAGE FRAIS**

In a bowl, combine 1¼ cups fromage frais with 2½ Tbsp lightly packed minced fresh dill, ½ tsp freshly ground black pepper and sea salt to taste.

Homemade cheese with the taste of mild ricotta and a breeze to make. What could be better?

Fromage frais is a fresh low-fat unripened cheese with a mousse-like texture and high moisture content. It is terrific as a base for poached or smoked salmon canapés, though Devin prefers to top the cheese with a poached shrimp or smoked trout (try the black pepper-dill version, too). You can also create a healthy, yummy vegetarian sandwich by spreading a generous layer of fromage frais on multigrain bread (page 30). Top it with thinly sliced cucumber, grated carrot, cooked beet slices, crunchy lettuce and a slice of ripe tomato.

Fromage frais, without any additions, will keep for three or four days in the refrigerator. Add the radish and chives just before serving, as they tend to overpower the cheese after a few hours.

To turn this into a dip, whisk in a little low-fat milk.

Pour the milk into a saucepan and bring it to a rolling boil. Remove from the heat and stir in the lemon juice. Cover and let sit for 2 hours.

Line a fine sieve with two layers of cheesecloth. Pour the liquid, which looks curdled, into the sieve. The curds (solids) will stay in the cheesecloth, and the whey (liquid) can be discarded. Sprinkle the curds with the salt and use the cheesecloth to squeeze out as much liquid as possible. Stop squeezing when the cheese starts to come through the cheesecloth. (If you squeeze too long and hard, the end product will be grainy.) Suspend the cheese in the cheesecloth in a bowl to allow more whey to drain and refrigerate for 1½ hours. Remove from the cheesecloth and refrigerate the cheese until ready to use. (Discard any liquid that drains from the cheese before using.)

Place the fromage frais in a bowl and fold in the radish, chives and pepper. Season with salt to taste.

Devin

BAKED LEMONY FETA CHEESE *with* THYME, ROSEMARY *and* BLACK PEPPER
(photo page 54)

I love it when I can take something that's simple and easy to find, like feta cheese, and doctor it up to make it unusual and delicious, with hardly any assembly required! This is one showstopper that will please a crowd. (I now make twice as much as I used to because it disappeared so fast.) Melted cheese, lemon, herbs and garlic. Serve it with a sliced baguette. So simple. (After all, it's the small victories that count!)

If you have the time, let your feta sit in a sieve for 30 minutes before baking to remove any extra water. Pat the feta dry and place in a small baking dish.

Preheat the oven to 450°F.

Drizzle the oil over the feta. Sprinkle with the lemon zest and pepper.

Place the garlic halves, cut side down, on top of the feta. Sprinkle with the thyme and rosemary.

Bake the feta for 20 minutes. Remove the garlic if you wish and sprinkle the cheese with the lemon juice. Serve directly from the baking dish.

SERVES 6 TO 8

1 lb (500 g) feta cheese

2 Tbsp extra-virgin olive oil

1 Tbsp lightly packed grated lemon zest, preferably organic

½ tsp freshly ground black pepper

2 cloves garlic, peeled and halved

½ tsp lightly packed finely chopped fresh thyme

½ tsp lightly packed finely chopped fresh rosemary

2 Tbsp freshly squeezed lemon juice

BEAUTY TIP

In the Buff:
Herbal Shower Scrub

Leave out the garlic and feta and you've got the basics for a great natural skin scrub. This one is especially good for rough areas like knees and elbows. Avoid on more sensitive areas.

Combine ½ cup kosher salt, ½ cup olive oil, 1 tsp grated lemon zest and ½ tsp minced fresh rosemary. Mix together and massage into callused areas in the shower. Rinse and pat dry.

Linda

TUNA

1 lb (500 g) sushi-grade tuna, in one
    piece, about 1½ inches thick

2 to 3 Tbsp vegetable oil

½ tsp kosher salt

¼ tsp freshly ground black pepper

3 Tbsp white sesame seeds

CILANTRO MINT CHUTNEY

2 bunches of fresh cilantro (about
    5 oz/150 g total)

1 bunch of fresh mint (about 2 oz/60 g)

1 large cooking onion, coarsely
    chopped

2-inch piece gingerroot, about 1 inch
    in diameter, peeled (page 113)

¼ to ½ tsp finely chopped hot
    green chili (e.g., serrano)

½ cup lime juice (fresh or bottled)

1½ Tbsp granulated sugar

1½ tsp kosher salt

⅛ tsp freshly ground black pepper

SESAME TUNA BITES
with CILANTRO MINT CHUTNEY

Thin slices of seared tuna with a cilantro-mint chutney make a great accompaniment to Devin's meatballs (page 55) on a tapas plate. You could also turn this into a light lunch; add an extra 8 oz (250 g) tuna and serve it on a bed of perfectly ripe tomatoes with a sprinkling of sweet onion slices.

Veena Aggarwal, who gave me the recipe for this bright, fresh-tasting chutney recipe, sometimes makes it with only cilantro leaves. If she wants a thicker, richer chutney she adds a bit of grated unsweetened coconut.

You will have more chutney (about 3 cups) than you'll need for the tuna. Try it with grilled salmon, grouper and snapper or steamed summer vegetables. The chutney should keep in your refrigerator for up to three days, and it can even be frozen without losing its brilliant green color.

To prepare the tuna, cut it in half down the middle. You should have two strips about 2 inches wide and 1½ inches thick.

Brush all sides of the tuna with oil. Sprinkle the two wide sides of each piece with salt and pepper. Pat a coating of sesame seeds on one wide side of each piece and brush the seeds very gently with a little oil.

Heat a cast-iron skillet over high heat. When the pan is hot, lay the sesame-crusted side of the tuna in the pan. Sear for 35 seconds, making sure the sesame seeds don't burn, then turn the fish and sear on the other side for 35 seconds. Use tongs to hold the fish while you sear the narrow sides for 15 to 20 seconds each. The tuna should be just seared around the sides and still be raw in the center.

Remove the tuna from the pan and let rest until it is at room temperature. (The tuna can be prepared a few hours ahead and refrigerated, but bring it to room temperature before serving.)

Meanwhile, to prepare the chutney, remove the roots but not the stems of the cilantro. Pull the leaves from the mint, discarding any wilted or bruised leaves.

Place the onion, ginger, chili, lime juice, sugar, salt and pepper in a food processor or blender and puree. Gradually pulse in the cilantro and mint. The chutney should be almost smooth but not runny and be a brilliant green color. Taste and add salt, sugar, lime or chili if necessary.

Cut the tuna into ¼-inch slices and arrange slightly overlapping on a serving dish. Drizzle with a small amount of chutney.

Devin

BABY LAMB MEATBALLS
with POMEGRANATE YOGURT DIP

The uses for sausages are endless. Don't laugh — it's true! In a tight jam I have used sausage meat in pasta sauce, on pizza, in soups and for meatballs. It's great because it's already seasoned and it comes in everything from turkey, to beef, to veal and pork . . . and, of course, lamb. (You can also use chicken or pork sausage in this recipe if you wish; just make sure the meatballs are cooked all the way through.)

This is so simple to make, and the luscious pile of pomegranate seeds looks really sexy. If you like, you can make the meatballs ahead of time and quickly heat them up in a 425°F oven for 5 to 6 minutes.

I serve the meatballs on fancy toothpicks, with the dip alongside.

For the dip, stir together the yogurt, salt, pepper and ½ Tbsp mint in a serving bowl. Pile the pomegranate seeds on top, sprinkle with the remaining ½ Tbsp mint and drizzle with oil.

For the meatballs, remove the sausage meat from the casings and mold into 1-inch balls.

In a large skillet, heat the oil over medium-high heat. Add the meatballs and brown evenly on all sides — about 7 minutes in total. To check for doneness, gently poke a knife into the center of a meatball. The center should be very slightly pink. Don't overcook them, or they will be tough. (You may need a bit more oil if you have to cook the meatballs in batches.)

Serve the meatballs with the dip.

POMEGRANATE YOGURT DIP

⅔ cup whole milk yogurt

½ tsp kosher salt

¼ tsp freshly ground black pepper

1 Tbsp lightly packed chopped fresh mint, divided

½ cup pomegranate seeds

1 tsp extra-virgin olive oil

MEATBALLS

3 large lamb sausages (about 1 lb/500 g total)

3 Tbsp olive oil

. . . .

KITCHEN HINT

POMEGRANATES

Look for pomegranates that feel heavy for their size and that have a glossy, burnished red skin.

To seed a pomegranate, cut the fruit in half and submerge a half at a time in a large bowl of cold water. Remove the seeds with your fingers. The inedible whitish membrane surrounding the seeds should rise to the surface of the water. Pick off any membrane that doesn't detach. Drain the seeds before using.

. . . .

What I really like about soup is that it's as at home on a picnic table as it is at an elegant dinner.

LINDA

SOUP'S ON

No wonder every culture eats soup. It's comforting, generally inexpensive and easy to make for a crowd.

DEVIN

Heirloom Tomato Soup with Baby Meatballs	58	Rustic Tomato Soup with Goat Cheese	60
Celery Root Puree with Chestnuts and Bacon	62	Lemon-scented Potato, Dill and Bacon Soup	65
Cauliflower Velouté with Walnuts and Benedictine Blue	66	Luscious Corn Soup with Basil Butter Crostini	67
Melon and Sparkling Wine Gazpacho with Grilled Shrimp and Mint	68	Carrot Gazpacho with Fresh Lime	71
Herbed White Bean Soup with Chorizo Sausage	72	Hearty Chicken, Barley and Tarragon Soup	74

Linda

SERVES 8 TO 10

HEIRLOOM TOMATO SOUP
with BABY MEATBALLS

SOUP

1½-lb (750 g) beef soup bone covered
    in some meat

2 Tbsp vegetable oil, divided

2 cooking onions, coarsely chopped

3 large stalks celery, coarsely chopped

1 leek, white and light-green part only,
    coarsely chopped

4 bay leaves

2 cloves garlic, chopped

3 large sprigs of fresh thyme

3 28-oz (796 mL) cans plum
    tomatoes, seeded, with juice

4 cups water

½ tsp kosher salt

¼ tsp freshly ground white pepper

½ cup warm 18% cream, optional

2 Tbsp lightly packed minced
    fresh parsley

MEATBALLS

1 lb (500 g) minced beef

1 large egg

¼ cup dry breadcrumbs (page 105)

3 Tbsp lightly packed minced
    fresh parsley

½ tsp kosher salt

⅛ tsp freshly ground black pepper

When my mother told me the story of her grandmother's tomato soup, I was determined to recreate it. She said one of her strongest childhood memories was going to her grandmother's house in Wetteren, Belgium, for Sunday lunch, opening the front door and being transported by the smell of her grandmother's soup. Over time, as I quizzed my mother, I learned more. A soup bone was used (for the best flavor ask your butcher to cut a prime rib bone lengthwise). She added celery and leeks, but no carrot. Twine was knotted around the meaty part of the bone to prevent the meat from falling into the soup. An hour and a half was the optimal cooking time, and the meatballs had to be made with beef, not veal, which has too delicate a taste. Her grandmother had not added cream, but my mother was ambivalent on the matter.

After a few tries, I invited my mom for lunch. This soup was on the stove when she arrived.

Serve it with a crusty baguette or multigrain bread (page 30).

For the soup, tie the meat to the soup bone using kitchen string.

Heat 1 Tbsp oil in a large pot over high heat. Brown the soup bone on all sides (this should take 5 to 6 minutes) and reserve.

Reduce the heat to medium and add the remaining 1 Tbsp oil. Add the onions, celery and leek. Sauté, stirring, for about 5 minutes, being careful not to brown the vegetables.

Add the bay leaves, garlic and thyme and continue to cook for another 3 minutes, but don't let the garlic brown.

Add the soup bone, tomatoes with their juice (you should have about 4 cups juice), water, salt and pepper. Bring to a low boil, cover and simmer gently for 1½ hours.

Remove the bone, bay leaves and thyme sprigs and puree the soup until completely smooth. (You may have to use a food mill or sieve.) Taste and add salt and pepper if needed. (If the tomatoes are very acidic, add a little granulated sugar.)

While the soup is cooking, prepare the meatballs. Combine the beef, egg, breadcrumbs, parsley, salt and pepper in a large bowl. Form into balls about ¾ inch in diameter (you should end up with about 40). Cover and refrigerate. Bring to room temperature before adding to the soup.

When ready to serve, heat the soup and gently add the meatballs. Simmer for about 5 to 6 minutes, or until the meatballs are cooked through. Stir in the cream, if you are using it.

Ladle the soup and meatballs into bowls and garnish each serving with parsley.

KITCHEN HINTS

GOING TO SEED: SEEDING CANNED TOMATOES

The best way to seed canned tomatoes is to put them through a food mill. Or, if you feel this would be just one more gadget filling your kitchen cupboards, simply cut the tomatoes in half and remove the seeds with your fingers.

ALL WASHED UP: CLEANING LEEKS

As leeks push themselves out of the ground, their "leaves" become havens for dirt. I trim off the dark-green leaves and roots, then slice them into rounds according to the recipe and throw them in a deep bowl of cold water. After they have sat for a few minutes, I swish them around to dislodge the last of the dirt. Dry them in a colander if you are using them in a soup, or on a tea towel if you want them really dry before sautéing.

Devin prefers to trim off the green tops and then slice down the middle of the leek through the light-green green and white part, leaving the roots intact. She then immerses them in cold water, shaking them once or twice until they are clean.

SERVES 2 TO 4

2 Tbsp extra-virgin olive oil

1 clove garlic, chopped

¾ cup drained and rinsed
 roasted red peppers

28-oz (796 mL) can plum tomatoes,
 with juice

1 cup chicken stock or vegetable stock

1 tsp kosher salt

¼ tsp freshly ground black pepper

2 tsp granulated sugar, optional

¼ cup coarsely crumbled goat cheese

. . . .

KITCHEN HINT

KITCHEN MAGIC:
THE WAND BLENDER

If you don't own a wand blender, a regular blender or a food processor, run, don't walk, to the nearest kitchen supply store and get yourself a wand blender, because once you have one, you'll never remember how you lived without it. They're not expensive, either.

I use mine to make vinaigrettes and salad dressings and to puree fruit and soups. Just be careful when you are pureeing hot soups — that's one reason I like to use a large pot, to contain hot splashes.

. . . .

RUSTIC TOMATO SOUP
with GOAT CHEESE

I really wish I had the time to make a decadent slow-simmered soup. I really wish I did. But let's be realistic. No one I know has time to make one of those soups (unless they've taken a "sick day" off work).

When I need a soup that serves up quickly and tastes great, this recipe is ideal. Who really wants to get lost in Prep World after a long day anyway? Even better is the fact that the three main ingredients can all be pulled from your pantry (I buy the roasted red peppers in a jar) and no measuring cups are required. This is especially important to me because, frankly, the thought of cleaning more dishes than I need to makes me pretty cranky.

This soup tastes like it took a few hours to make, so keep this little secret to yourself. It is homemade, after all! It's perfect for a quick dinner with a nice green salad and a good baguette.

Don't skip the goat cheese garnish. (This soup is so healthy and low in fat that you can go a little crazy in the cheese department.)

Heat the olive oil in a large pot over medium heat. Add the garlic and sauté for 1 to 2 minutes, just until softened but not brown.

Add the red peppers, tomatoes and juice, stock, salt and pepper. (Don't worry about chopping anything at this stage, because you will need to puree everything later.) Simmer, uncovered, for 15 minutes, stirring occasionally.

Remove from the heat and puree until you have a nice smooth texture. If the soup tastes a bit acidic, add the sugar a teaspoon at a time to balance out the flavors.

Serve in nice big bowls and add as much crumbled goat cheese as you like.

Linda

SERVES 8 TO 10

2 Tbsp vegetable oil

1 cooking onion, chopped

1 large clove garlic, chopped

2 carrots, peeled and cut
   in ½-inch pieces

7 stalks celery, plus leaves from the
   whole bunch of celery, cut
   in 1-inch pieces

1 celery root (about 1 lb/500 g),
   peeled and cut in ½-inch pieces

2 bay leaves

1½ tsp lightly packed fresh thyme

2 tsp kosher salt

½ tsp freshly ground black pepper

8 cups chicken stock

¼ cup 18% cream

6 thick slices bacon, diced

20 cooked chestnuts (about 3 to
   4 oz/90 to 125 g), coarsely crumbled

CELERY ROOT PUREE
with CHESTNUTS *and* BACON

Celery root, often called celeriac, is a root vegetable with a delicate celery taste. Delicious roasted or pureed in a soup, it's low in calories but rich in taste. Although a soup puree usually contains butter, I've omitted it here to let the chestnuts and bacon shine thorough.

I love this soup to start a fall or winter dinner. Duck (page 144) or pork chops (page 150) would make a good main. You can also cook more soup than you need, as it freezes well.

Vacuum-packed cooked chestnuts can be found in specialty stores and in the international section of most supermarkets.

Add the oil and onions to a large pot and heat over medium heat. Sauté for a few minutes, or until soft, taking care not to let the onions brown.

Add the garlic, carrots, celery stalks and leaves, celery root, bay leaves, thyme, salt and pepper. Sauté for 4 minutes.

Add the chicken stock, bring to a low boil and simmer, partially covered, for about 30 minutes, or until the celery root is soft.

Remove the soup from the heat, remove the bay leaves and cool. Add the cream and puree. Taste and adjust the seasonings if necessary.

Before serving, sauté the bacon in a skillet until crisp. Drain on a paper towel.

Reheat the soup. Drop some bacon and chestnuts into the bottom of each bowl before ladling in the soup.

BEAUTY TIP

My Grandmother's Facial Scrub

My grandmother had the world's most beautiful peaches-and-cream skin. She lived into her late eighties, looking at least twenty years younger than her age. Twice a week she put a spoonful of salt into the palm of her hand and moistened it with water. She then gently rubbed it in a circular motion over her face, rinsed it off with cool water and patted on an inexpensive face cream. She recommended this simple scrub to all her friends with oily and normal skin.

KITCHEN HINT

CHESTNUTS

You can buy cooked chestnuts in vacuum packs (they have a slightly more crumbly texture and sweeter flavor than the ones you roast yourself), or roast your own. Look for fresh unshelled chestnuts with shiny uncracked and unblemished shells. They are in the markets from September to February.

Cut a cross in one side of each chestnut, making sure you cut through both the hard outside shell and the thin fibrous layer of skin beneath it.

Place on a baking sheet and bake at 375°F for 25 minutes. Cool and peel off the shell and second layer of skin to expose the pale golden flesh of the nut.

Devin

LEMON-SCENTED POTATO, DILL *and* BACON SOUP

I absolutely love Mom's celery root soup with chestnuts and bacon (page 62). It's smoky and luxurious. My creamy soup has a similar end result but is easier and more accessible. Just potatoes, dill, lemon and bacon — all ingredients that you can find at your local grocery store. If you want to make a meal of it, this is also a perfect base for a hearty fish chowder.

Cook the bacon in a small skillet over medium-low heat for 5 to 7 minutes, or until browned and crisp. Drain on a paper towel and set aside.

Combine the stock, garlic, potatoes, celery, salt and pepper in a large pot and bring to a low boil. Simmer for 15 to 20 minutes, or until the potatoes are tender.

Puree the soup until smooth.

Return the pot to the stove over medium heat and stir in the lemon zest and cream. Simmer for 5 minutes to incorporate all the flavors.

Just before serving, stir in the dill and garnish each serving with bacon. Serve with a lemon wedge.

DEVIN'S FISH CHOWDER
Bring the finished soup to a low boil. Add 8 oz (250 g) cleaned and deveined jumbo shrimp (about 12) and 8 oz (250 g) halibut cut in 1-inch cubes. Cook for 3 to 4 minutes, or until the shrimp and halibut are tender (Mom sometimes adds a dozen or so clams that she has cooked separately).
   Serves 6 to 8.

SERVES 6

5 slices bacon, cut in ½-inch pieces

4 cups chicken stock

2 cloves garlic, chopped

3 large Yukon Gold potatoes (about 1½ lbs/750 g), peeled and cut in 1-inch pieces

2 stalks celery, finely chopped

1½ tsp kosher salt

¼ tsp freshly ground black pepper

1 Tbsp lightly packed grated lemon zest, preferably organic (about 1 medium)

½ cup 35% (whipping) cream

2 tsp lightly packed chopped fresh dill

1 lemon, cut in wedges, for garnish

. . . .
KITCHEN HINT

DELICATE DILL
Don't add fresh dill to a cooked dish until just before serving. Dill loses its flavor and color in hot food if it sits for too long.
. . . .

Linda

CAULIFLOWER VELOUTÉ *with* WALNUTS *and* BENEDICTINE BLUE

SERVES 6

1 large cauliflower (2 lbs/1 kg), trimmed and coarsely chopped

4½ cups whole milk

3 cloves garlic, peeled and cut in half

¼ cup coarsely chopped walnuts

1 tsp kosher salt

⅛ tsp freshly ground white pepper

¼ cup golden raisins

⅓ cup crumbled Benedictine Blue cheese

I took a leaf out of Devin's book – see her fabulous corn soup – to make this easy but creamy (and with no cream in it) soup. This isn't strictly speaking a velouté, which normally includes a white stock made from chicken, veal or fish and eggs and cream. Instead, this quick-to-make low-calorie version lets you indulge in the cheese garnish. Benedictine Blue is a mouth-watering, moist and slightly crumbly cheese from Quebec. You can use Stilton as a substitute if this gorgeous cheese isn't available in your area.

Combine the cauliflower, milk and garlic in a large saucepan. Cover and bring to a low boil. Simmer for about 10 minutes, or until the cauliflower is soft.

Meanwhile, place the walnuts in a small dry skillet and cook, stirring, over medium heat for about 5 minutes.

Cool the cauliflower mixture slightly and spoon all but ¾ cup liquid into a food processor. Add the salt and pepper and puree until smooth (you may have to do this in batches). Add liquid until you have the consistency you want. The soup can be kept refrigerated for up to two days.

Reheat the soup. Taste and adjust the seasonings if necessary. Ladle into individual bowls and top each serving with raisins, walnuts and cheese.

Devin

LUSCIOUS CORN SOUP
with BASIL BUTTER CROSTINI

I learned this recipe from one of North America's great culinary teachers, Mary Risley, owner of the Tante Marie Cooking School in San Francisco. I have known Mary through my dad for years, and she cooked this soup for me when I stayed at her Connecticut home for the weekend. It is the easiest soup you will ever make and one of the most delicious. The richness is so intense, it's almost impossible to believe that it is virtually fat free. All you need is fresh corn and skim milk! I recommend making this soup in the summer when corn is at its peak. I love it served with the crostini, which act like giant croutons, soaking up all the wonderful summer flavor of the soup.

For the soup, use a large box grater to grate each ear of raw corn into a large dish. You should end up with about 2⅓ cups grated corn.

Heat the oil in a large pot over medium-low heat. Add the corn and sauté for 1 minute.

Add the milk, salt and pepper, bring to a low boil and simmer for 15 minutes.

To prepare the crostini, combine the butter, basil, salt and pepper in a small bowl. Spread over toasted pieces of baguette.

Serve the soup and float 2 crostini on each serving.

SERVES 4

SOUP

10 corn on the cob, shucked

1 Tbsp extra-virgin olive oil

3½ cups skim milk

1¼ tsp kosher salt

½ tsp freshly ground black pepper

BASIL BUTTER CROSTINI

¼ cup unsalted butter,
   at room temperature

1 Tbsp lightly packed finely
   chopped fresh basil

Pinch of kosher salt

Pinch of freshly ground black pepper

8 slices baguette, about ½ inch
   thick, toasted

Linda

SOUP

6 cups honeydew melon pieces,
  cut in 1-inch chunks

¾ cup Prosecco or other dry
  sparkling white wine

3 Tbsp freshly squeezed lemon juice

½ tsp kosher salt

⅛ tsp freshly ground white pepper

SHRIMP

8 jumbo shrimp, peeled and deveined

1 Tbsp extra-virgin olive oil

1 Tbsp freshly squeezed lemon juice

¼ tsp kosher salt

⅛ tsp freshly ground white pepper

1 to 2 Tbsp lightly packed shredded
  fresh mint, for garnish

MELON *and* SPARKLING WINE GAZPACHO *with* GRILLED SHRIMP *and* MINT

You might think that a soup made with melon and sparkling wine would be sweet and cloying, but that's not the case with this light and flavorful gazpacho. A good squeeze of lemon juice, the warm grilled shrimp and the touch of mint make this a sophisticated starter on a warm summer evening. I have made this soup with cantaloupe, too, and when I'm feeling very ambitious I split the recipe in two and use both kinds of melons. I put the two purees in different pitchers and pour them into individual bowls at the same time. The result is beautiful bowl of gazpacho that is orange on one side and a lovely green on the other.

For the soup, puree the melon. (A blender will give you a smoother consistency, but a food processor or wand blender will also do the job.) Transfer to a bowl and whisk in the sparkling wine, lemon juice, salt and pepper. Taste and adjust the seasonings (add more lemon juice if your melon is extra sweet). Refrigerate until cool.

For the shrimp, combine the shrimp, oil, lemon juice, salt and pepper in a bowl and toss.

Heat a grill pan or cast-iron skillet over high heat until very hot. Add the shrimp and cook for 1½ minutes per side. Remove from the pan and, when cool enough to handle, slice in half lengthwise.

Ladle the cool soup into bowls. Mound 4 pieces of warm shrimp in the middle of each bowl and sprinkle with the mint. Serve immediately.

Devin

CARROT GAZPACHO
with FRESH LIME

Just picture it — a tangy chilled carrot soup with a spritz of lime, a Corona, my Argentinian flank steak (page 154) and Mom's tomato and zucchini gratin (page 166). Need I go on?

   This soup offers all you could want in a starter for a summer meal. It's fresh, bright, cool and looks totally amazing. No offense to my good old friend the tomato gazpacho, but this soup will make you realize the humble carrot is a force to be reckoned with.

Heat the oil in a large pot over medium heat. Add the onion and sauté for 4 to 5 minutes, or until softened.

Add the garlic, carrots, celery, salt and pepper. Increase the heat to medium-high and cook, stirring, for 5 minutes.

Add the stock and bring to a low boil. Simmer, covered, for 15 to 20 minutes, or until the carrots are cooked through and tender.

Remove from the heat and add the vinegar, five-spice powder and the cream, if you are using it.

Allow the mixture to cool and puree it until very smooth. Refrigerate the soup until chilled. Stir in the lime juice before serving and sprinkle with a light dusting of zest.

. . . .

KITCHEN HINT

THE TRUTH ABOUT BABY CARROTS
When I found out that those cute and convenient bags of pre-washed and peeled little carrots are usually the peeled-down cores of misshapen or even rotten large carrots, I started to buy real carrots, even though it takes a bit of extra time to peel them. (I try to buy the ones with the green tops; not those big "horse" carrots that come in the bags.)

. . . .

SERVES 8

2 Tbsp extra-virgin olive oil

½ cup finely chopped cooking onion

1 large clove garlic, chopped

2½ lbs (1 kg) carrots, peeled and coarsely chopped

1 stalk celery, chopped

2 tsp kosher salt

½ tsp freshly ground black pepper

4 cups chicken stock or vegetable stock

1 Tbsp cider vinegar

½ tsp five-spice powder

½ cup 10% (half-and-half) cream, optional

¼ cup freshly squeezed lime juice

2 tsp lightly packed grated lime zest, preferably organic

Linda

3 Tbsp extra-virgin olive oil

½ cup coarsely chopped leek,
    white part only

⅓ cup diced carrot

⅓ cup diced celery

2 cloves garlic, finely chopped

¼ tsp kosher salt

⅛ tsp freshly ground black pepper

2 small bay leaves

1 Tbsp lightly packed finely chopped
    fresh sage, or ½ tsp dried

1 Tbsp lightly packed finely chopped
    fresh rosemary, or ½ tsp dried

4 cups chicken stock

3 19-oz (540 mL) cans white
    kidney beans, rinsed and drained

SAUSAGES

2 tsp extra-virgin olive oil

2 spicy air-dried chorizo sausages
    (about 8 oz/250 g)

3 Tbsp lightly packed coarsely
    chopped flat-leaf parsley

HERBED WHITE BEAN SOUP
with CHORIZO SAUSAGE

Although this soup tastes like it's been on the stove for hours, you can have it on the table in less than 45 minutes. It's important that the beans be well rinsed. This will remove most of the sodium and also reduce the complex sugars that lead to gassiness. If you can't find air-dried chorizo, use cooked fresh chorizo or other pork or lamb sausage (you'll need about 12 oz/375 g fresh sausage). A couple of handfuls of chopped kale can also be added during the last few minutes of cooking. Serve with warm focaccia.

Warm the oil slightly in a large saucepan over medium heat. Add the leek, carrot, celery, garlic, salt and pepper and sauté for 4 to 5 minutes, or until the vegetables are tender but not colored. Add the bay leaves, sage and rosemary and cook for another minute.

Pour in the stock, bring to a low boil and simmer for 5 minutes. Add the beans and simmer for an additional 5 minutes. Remove the bay leaves. Taste and adjust the seasonings, adding salt and pepper if necessary.

Meanwhile, to prepare the sausages, heat the oil in a separate skillet over medium-high heat. Add the sausages and cook for a few minutes until crisp and warmed through. Slice into ¼-inch rounds.

Remove 3 cups beans from the soup and puree. Return to the pot with the sausages and simmer for 5 minutes. Ladle into bowls and sprinkle with parsley.

Devin

SERVES 6

3 cups water

1 cup pearl barley

3 Tbsp extra-virgin olive oil

3 cloves garlic, finely chopped

¾ cup finely chopped cooking onion
 (1 small)

2 stalks celery, finely chopped

2 carrots, peeled and finely chopped

1½ tsp kosher salt

¼ tsp freshly ground black pepper

1 lb (500 g) boneless, skinless
 chicken breasts (about 2 large),
 cut in ½-inch pieces

4 cups chicken stock

2 Tbsp lightly packed finely chopped
 fresh tarragon

¼ cup 35% (whipping) cream,
 optional

HEARTY CHICKEN, BARLEY
and TARRAGON SOUP

I'm always sad to say goodbye to summer, but this comforting soup gets me through the winter months. It is essentially a more exciting, healthier and heartier version of good old chicken noodle soup. I keep any leftovers in the fridge for a day or so, where the barley thickens the soup even more, turning it into a kind of barley risotto that is absolutely delicious as well.

Serve this in large bowls with a crisp green salad on the side.

Bring the water to a low boil in a saucepan. Add the barley and simmer with the lid ajar, stirring occasionally, for 50 to 60 minutes, or until tender.

Meanwhile, heat the oil in a large pot over medium heat. Add the garlic, onion, celery, carrots, salt and pepper and sauté for 5 minutes.

Add the chicken and cook, stirring, until just cooked through – about 5 to 6 minutes.

Pour in the stock and bring to a simmer.

Add the cooked barley, tarragon and cream, if you are using it. Simmer for another 10 minutes to incorporate all the flavors.

. . . .

KITCHEN HINT

BARLEY

Barley is an ancient grain and has been discovered in archeological sites dating back more than 10,000 years. Only 10 percent of the crop is used in cooking; about one third is used in the brewing industry and most is used to feed livestock.

The most common forms of barley are hulled barley (only the outermost hull has been removed), pot barley (stripped of the outer hull and bran layer) and pearl barley (the most refined, with the hull, bran and endosperm removed).

. . . .

In this day and age of soggy take-out salads, I like to take the time to look for interesting and unique ingredients. After all, you can get an overdressed Caesar salad anywhere.

LINDA

THE LIGHTER SIDE: SALADS

As a starter or a meal unto itself, for me a salad is meant to be fast, fresh, simple, healthy and, of course, delicious.

DEVIN

SERVES 4 TO 6

CANDIED WALNUTS

1 cup shelled walnut halves

⅓ cup maple syrup

SALAD

3 heads Boston lettuce
(about 8 oz/250g each), pale-green
leaves only, separated

2 crisp Fuyu persimmons, peeled and
cut in ¼-inch wedges

1 Tbsp plus 1 tsp Minus 8 vinegar,
or 1 Tbsp red wine vinegar mixed
with 1 tsp honey

¼ tsp kosher salt

2 Tbsp extra-virgin olive oil

⅛ tsp freshly ground black pepper

12 to 14 curls Parmigiano Reggiano
(about 1½ oz/45 g)

. . . .

KITCHEN HINT

PERFECT PERSIMMONS

Buy persimmons that have smooth,
bright-orange glossy skin. Store them
at room temperature until ripe, and
then refrigerate.

Use crisp, flat-topped Fuyu persimmons in salads. The domed Hachiya
persimmons are best used very ripe as a
puree in puddings and cakes.

. . . .

SWEET GREENS *with* PERSIMMONS, CANDIED WALNUTS *and* PARMIGIANO REGGIANO

There are some special ingredients in this festive salad — Minus 8
vinegar from the Niagara wine region in Ontario, persimmons,
top-quality Parmigiano Reggiano and delicious candied walnuts.
All the ingredients can be prepared hours ahead. If persimmons
are out of season (they are widely available from September
through December), try figs, nectarines or plums. A combination
of Boston lettuce and mâche (lamb's lettuce) is delicious, too.

I like to serve this plated individually as a light appetizer or between the main course and dessert.

Preheat the oven to 350°F.

For the walnuts, heat a large skillet over medium heat. Add
the walnuts and cook for about 1 minute, shaking the pan
constantly. Add the maple syrup and cook for 15 to 20 seconds,
or just until the syrup disappears, making sure not to burn
the nuts.

Shake the walnuts onto an oiled baking sheet and bake for
about 5 to 7 minutes, or until the maple syrup looks like brown
sugar. Immediately remove from the baking sheet and cool.

For the salad, combine the lettuce and persimmons in a bowl.

Whisk together the vinegar and salt in a small bowl. Set aside
for 5 minutes to allow the salt to dissolve. Whisk in the oil and
then the pepper. Taste and adjust the seasonings if necessary.
(The amount of dressing is small since the greens are delicate
and you only want to lightly coat each leaf.) If you prefer a more
dressed salad, double the vinaigrette ingredients. Extra vinaigrette
will keep for one week.

Toss the lettuce and persimmons with the dressing. Mound on
individual plates and top with the walnuts and cheese.

Devin

WATERCRESS *with* RED GRAPES *and* PECORINO SHARDS

I adore salads with fruit in them. Mangoes, peaches, raspberries or grapes can all really liven up a traditional green salad. Mom's persimmon salad hits all the right notes, but becomes a little tricky when persimmons are hard to find.

In this recipe, I use readily available red grapes to balance the peppery watercress, and the Pecorino adds the perfect saltiness. Lucky for me, I had these things lying around the house after a weekend cocktail party!

This is a gorgeous-looking salad, so if you're aiming to impress, this is the perfect choice.

If you can't find or don't like watercress (supposedly great for strengthening the lungs and purging toxins from the body), then arugula is a good substitute. Parmesan will also work well if Pecorino Romano isn't available.

Whisk together the mustard, honey, salt, pepper and lemon juice in a bowl. Slowly drizzle in the oil while continuously whisking. Set aside.

Place the watercress in a large bowl and toss with the dressing. Sprinkle the grapes and cheese over the watercress.

SERVES 4

1 tsp Dijon mustard

1 tsp liquid honey

¼ tsp kosher salt

¼ tsp freshly ground black pepper

1½ Tbsp freshly squeezed lemon juice

3 Tbsp extra-virgin olive oil

5 to 6 oz (150 to 175 g) watercress, trimmed (4 or 5 large handfuls)

¾ cup seedless red grapes, cut in half

2 oz (60 g) Pecorino Romano cheese, shaved

Linda

4 cups shelled green peas

1 cup shelled fava, lima or
   edamame beans

2 slices pancetta or bacon,
   about ¼ inch thick

2 Tbsp finely chopped radish

¼ cup peeled, seeded and finely
   chopped English cucumber

1 green onion, white and light-green
   part only, finely chopped

1 Tbsp freshly squeezed lemon juice

1 Tbsp lightly packed grated lemon
   zest (about 1 medium),
   preferably organic

1 Tbsp extra-virgin olive oil

Kosher salt and freshly ground
   black pepper to taste

MIXED GREEN PEA SALAD
with PANCETTA *and* RADISH

This salad is designed to let the taste of fresh spring peas shine
through. That's why all the other ingredients are finely chopped
and the dressing is kept to a minimum. Although I like to make
this with the first peas of the season, when the fresh peas become
bigger and starchy I switch to frozen baby peas, which are often
sweeter and more tender.

   This taste of spring is especially beautiful garnished with fresh
green pea sprouts.

Bring a saucepan of salted water to a boil. Add the peas and
beans and cook for about 3 minutes, or until just tender. Plunge
them into cold water to stop the cooking process and retain the
color. Drain.

Dice the pancetta and sauté in a small skillet until crisp. Drain
on a paper towel.

In a serving bowl, combine the peas, beans, pancetta, radish,
cucumber and green onion.

Whisk together the lemon juice, zest and oil in a small bowl.
Add salt and pepper to taste. Pour over the vegetables and toss.
Taste and adjust the seasonings, adding a little more lemon
juice and oil if you prefer a more dressed salad.

COOL AS A CUCUMBER
For a refreshing drink on a hot day or after a workout, fill
a tall pitcher with water and ten thin slices of both lemon and
cucumber. Let sit for 10 to 15 minutes and add a few ice cubes.

Devin

ITALIAN CHICKPEA, TUNA *and* PARSLEY SALAD

My friend Justine made this salad for lunch when we spent a weekend with some girlfriends at my parents' country house. It was so simple, fast and delicious. She just whipped out a couple of cans of white tuna, some canned chickpeas and fresh crunchy celery and dressed it with lots of lemon and olive oil. I've just added a little fresh parsley and some red pepper flakes to spice it up a bit.

Toss the chickpeas, tuna, celery, onion, parsley, lemon juice, oil, salt, hot pepper flakes and pepper together in a large bowl and allow to marinate for up to 30 minutes before serving.

BEAUTY TIP

Kissing Sweet

My nana once told me that if I wanted to be kissing sweet, I should chew on fresh parsley, a natural breath freshener, after eating a meal heavy on garlic or onions.

SERVES 4

19-oz (540 mL) can chickpeas, rinsed and drained

6-oz (170 g) can flaked water-packed white tuna, drained

3 stalks celery, cut in ¼-inch pieces

¼ red onion, finely sliced in rings

3 Tbsp lightly packed minced fresh parsley

¼ cup freshly squeezed lemon juice (about 1 medium)

2 Tbsp extra-virgin olive oil

1 tsp kosher salt

½ tsp hot red pepper flakes

¼ tsp freshly ground black pepper

Linda

SHAVED FENNEL, ORANGE, SWEET ONION *and* AVOCADO *with* ARUGULA

SERVES 6

4 thin slices sweet onion,
    separated in rings

4 large oranges

1 avocado

⅓ small fennel bulb
    (about 3½ oz/100 g),
    cut horizontally in slices
    about ⅛ to ¼ inch thick
    and broken up into rings,
    fronds reserved

3 to 4 oz (90 to 125 g) baby arugula
    (about 3 cups lightly packed)

1 Tbsp freshly squeezed orange juice

2½ tsp freshly squeezed lemon juice

½ tsp kosher salt

2 Tbsp extra-virgin olive oil

½ tsp freshly ground black pepper

This salad looks beautiful on the plate and takes just minutes to prepare. The tangy sweetness of the orange, the crunchy fennel and onion and the creamy avocado create a taste sensation from the very first bite. Although it's perfect as an appetizer, Devin and I also like it as a light lunch served with a chunk of Parmigiano Reggiano, a few slices of prosciutto and some sourdough bread.

Soak the onions in cold water for 30 minutes to reduce the bite. Drain and pat dry.

Cut the top and bottom off each orange. Rest the flat surface of the orange on a chopping board. Following the contour of the orange, cut off the rind and pith from top to bottom. Cut the oranges into ¼-inch slices and layer, slightly overlapping, on a large serving dish.

Peel and pit the avocado and slice it thinly.

Arrange the fennel, onion rings and avocado over the oranges in separate layers. Crown with arugula.

Combine the orange juice, lemon juice and salt in a small bowl and let the mixture sit for 5 minutes to dissolve the salt. Whisk in the oil and pepper. Taste and adjust the seasonings, adding oil if necessary.

Drizzle the vinaigrette over the arugula and top with a few fennel fronds before serving.

Devin

SPICY GREEN MANGO SALAD *with* PINEAPPLE, PEANUTS *and* CILANTRO

SERVES 4

I always order green mango salad when I go to a Thai restaurant. I love its sweet, sour, salty freshness and all the bright colors. You'll find a few more ingredients here than in a traditional recipe.

1 unripe mango, or 2 small green mangoes

If you are able to find real green mangoes (the ones that actually stay green) from a Chinese grocer, all the better, but I often use a large unripe Haden mango instead, which is a good substitute. This would be an amazing accompaniment for my grilled squid (page 135) or any grilled fish.

4 slices fresh pineapple (about ½ inch thick)

1 handful green beans, trimmed (about 2 oz/60 g)

Peel the mango and cut it into sticks about ¼ inch thick. Place the mango in a large bowl.

1 green onion, white and light-green part only, thinly sliced

Cut the pineapple rounds into ¼-inch-thick sticks and add to the bowl. (You won't be able to get all of your pieces the same shape, but that's fine.)

6 cherry tomatoes, quartered

1 small handful fresh cilantro, coarsely chopped

Slice the green beans on a sharp angle into ½-inch pieces and add to the mango and pineapple.

½ tsp hot red pepper flakes

⅓ cup coarsely chopped salted peanuts

Add the green onion, tomatoes, cilantro, hot pepper flakes, peanuts, salt, pepper and lime juice and toss gently. (I like to hold back a little bit of the cilantro and peanuts and sprinkle them on top for a garnish.)

½ tsp kosher salt

¼ tsp freshly ground black pepper

1 Tbsp freshly squeezed lime juice

SERVES 6

1 lb (500 g) butternut squash, peeled, seeded and cut in ½-inch slices (about 12 oz/375 g after seeding and peeling)

2 tsp extra-virgin olive oil

3 Tbsp liquid honey, warm, divided

½ cup chopped walnuts

2 Tbsp freshly squeezed lemon juice

2 Tbsp walnut oil

½ tsp kosher salt

¼ tsp freshly ground black pepper

6 to 8 oz (175 to 250 g) mâche or baby mixed greens (about 6 cups lightly packed)

½ cup crumbled feta (about 3 oz/90 g)

KITCHEN HINT

WALNUT OIL

Walnut oil is more expensive than vegetable oils and olive oils because of the difficulty of extracting oil from the nut. It also has a shorter shelf life and should be stored in the refrigerator once opened. It is not suitable for cooking at high temperatures, and is usually used to add flavor to cooked foods and salad dressings.

HONEY-ROASTED SQUASH
with CRUMBLED FETA *and* WALNUTS

This is a wonderful autumn salad that's a snap to put together. If I roast the squash a day ahead I can assemble the salad in 10 minutes — the time it takes to warm the squash in a 350°F oven. I like to serve Devin's grilled shrimp (page 138) next and finish with an almond tart (page 196).

Don't overdress the mâche. It is very delicate and wilts easily.

Preheat the oven to 400°F.

Toss the squash and olive oil in a large bowl. Spread on a parchment-lined baking sheet and lightly brush with half the honey. Bake for 15 minutes. Turn and brush with the remaining honey. Bake for another 15 minutes, or until the squash is cooked through.

While the squash is baking, place the walnuts in a small ovenproof dish and bake for about 5 minutes, or until lightly toasted.

Whisk together the lemon juice, walnut oil, salt and pepper in a small bowl.

Toss the mâche with the vinaigrette in a large bowl and place on serving plates. Top with 3 to 5 slices of squash. Sprinkle with walnuts and feta and a touch more salt and pepper. Serve while the squash is still warm.

Devin

CRUNCHY BASIL-FRIED TOMATOES
with GOAT CHEESE

On a warm summer day, when I don't want to turn on the oven, I love making these quick, flash-fried tomatoes. This is the only time I will ever suggest using unripe or even green tomatoes. The firm structure prevents them from turning to absolute mush when they are fried. Look for large beefsteak or heirloom tomatoes that are still very firm to the touch and slightly yellow or green in color.

You will be amazed at how well the basil leaf sticks to the tomato. It's gorgeously crispy and fragrant, as well as beautiful to look at. You could serve a couple of these as a side dish, or on a bed of arugula for a lovely warm salad.

Mix together the flour, cornmeal and pepper in a shallow dish.

Lightly beat the egg white in a separate shallow dish.

Trim the tops and bottoms from the tomatoes. Cut the tomatoes into slices about ½ inch thick (you should have about 8 slices).

One at a time, dip a slice of tomato into the egg white to coat, letting any extra egg white drip off. Press a basil leaf on one side of the tomato. Press the tomato, basil side down, into the flour mixture to coat. Turn and coat the other side, tapping off any extra flour.

Heat the oil in a large skillet over medium-high heat. Add the tomatoes basil side down (you may have to do this in batches; add a little more oil for the second batch if necessary). Fry on each side for 1½ to 2 minutes, or until golden and crispy. Remove and sprinkle with salt and goat cheese. Eat immediately.

SERVES 4

¼ cup all-purpose flour

¼ cup fine cornmeal

¼ tsp freshly ground black pepper

1 large egg white

2 large unripe beefsteak
   or heirloom tomatoes

8 fresh basil leaves

2 Tbsp extra-virgin olive oil

Kosher salt to taste

¼ cup crumbled goat cheese

BEAUTY TIP

Basil Lavender Facial Steam

Basil and lavender are natural relaxants. Give this facial steam a try after a hard day.

Fill a bowl with 3 cups boiling water, a handful of fresh basil and 1 Tbsp dried lavender buds. Let steep for 1 minute.

Clean your face and lower it over the infused water. Drape a towel over your head and most of the bowl. The smell will soothe your senses and the steam will clear your sinuses and pores. Try to stay under the towel for a few minutes.

Immediately splash your skin with cool water. Apply a toner and face cream.

Linda

1½ cups dried wheat berries,
 rinsed and drained

1 Tbsp unsalted butter

1 tsp kosher salt

3½ cups water

⅓ cup slivered almonds
 (about 1½ oz/45 g)

15 to 20 dried apricots
 (about 4 oz/125 g), each cut
 in 6 pieces

1 green onion, white and light-green
 part only, finely chopped

2 Tbsp lightly packed finely chopped
 fresh chives

¼ cup freshly squeezed orange juice

2 Tbsp almond oil or
 extra-virgin olive oil

½ tsp kosher salt

¼ tsp freshly ground black pepper

. . . .

KITCHEN HINT

WHEAT BERRIES

Wheat berries are whole husked wheat
kernels with the bran and germ intact.
Because they are whole grains, they have
a high oil content, so buy just the amount
you need and store it in the refrigerator.

  Bulgur, the main ingredient in tab-
bouleh, is made up of partially hulled,
cooked, dried and milled wheat berries.

. . . .

APRICOT *and* TOASTED ALMOND WHEAT BERRY SALAD

I love the nutty flavor and texture of wheat berries. They're a natural for a hearty but healthy salad. This salad is more spring or autumn fare than Devin's wonderfully light couscous salad. If you can't find almond oil, use a mild-tasting extra-virgin olive oil.

  You may want to buy organic dried apricots, untreated by sulfur dioxide. They are available in health food and specialty stores. Unlike the peachy-orange color of regular dried apricots, organic apricots are a pale brown.

Cover the wheat berries with water and let sit for 30 minutes. Drain well.

Melt the butter in a large, deep saucepan. Add the wheat berries and salt and sauté, stirring, for about 1 minute, or until all the grains are coated with butter.

Add the water to the saucepan, cover, bring to a low boil and simmer for about 1 hour, or until the wheat berries are cooked through. Drain off any excess water and allow them to cool for 30 minutes.

While the wheat berries are cooking, toast the almonds in a dry skillet over medium heat. Cook, stirring, for about 4 minutes, or until they are golden brown.

Combine the wheat berries, almonds, apricots, green onion and chives in a serving bowl.

Whisk the orange juice, oil, salt and pepper together in a small bowl. Toss the salad with the dressing. (Use more juice and oil if you like a more dressed salad.)

Devin

SUMMER COUSCOUS SALAD *with* FETA, ARTICHOKES, RAISINS *and* CHIVES

SERVES 6 TO 8

This might seem like a slightly odd combination of flavors, but trust me, it is absolutely delicious! It's always good to have a few recipes like this up your sleeve for unexpected vegetarian visitors. Instant couscous is an absolute pantry staple, and it's great to use when you find yourself doing a bit of a fridge purge and need to use up leftover veggies, meat or cheese. Just toss it all together with some olive oil, salt and pepper, and you have an instant meal.

Place the raisins in a small bowl or measuring cup and cover with boiling water. Soak for 15 minutes. Drain well.

Meanwhile, place the couscous in a large bowl and cover with 2 cups boiling water. Cover with a lid or dish towel and let sit for 5 minutes. Fluff with a fork.

Add the oil, drained raisins, artichokes, feta, chives, garlic, salt, pepper, parsley and lemon juice and toss together.

¾ cup raisins

1½ cups instant (quick-cooking) couscous

2 cups boiling water

3 Tbsp extra-virgin olive oil

1¼ cups drained and quartered water-packed artichoke hearts

1 cup cubed feta cheese (about 6 oz/175 g)

2 Tbsp lightly packed finely chopped fresh chives

¼ clove garlic, grated

½ tsp kosher salt

¼ tsp freshly ground black pepper

¼ cup lightly packed coarsely chopped fresh flat-leaf parsley

3 Tbsp freshly squeezed lemon juice

Linda

LEMON SALMON TARTARE LAYERED
with SPICY WHIPPED AVOCADO

SERVES 4

LEMON SALMON

12 oz (375 g) boneless,
  skinless salmon, organic or
  wild if possible

4 large sprigs of fresh chervil

2 tsp capers

1 Tbsp freshly squeezed lemon juice

½ tsp kosher salt

¼ tsp freshly ground white pepper

SPICY WHIPPED AVOCADO

2 avocados

1 Tbsp coarsely chopped sweet onion

1 Tbsp finely chopped jalapeño

2 Tbsp freshly squeezed lime juice

⅛ tsp cayenne pepper

⅛ tsp kosher salt

⅛ tsp freshly ground white pepper

I had a version of this pretty and mouth-watering dish while staying at a house on the coast of France just north of Biarritz. We sat on the terrace looking out over a long white sand beach and ate it accompanied by a local apéritif. The pale pink salmon is layered in a glass between spoonfuls of soft green avocado, making for a luscious look. In France this presentation is called a *verrine* and is usually reserved for desserts. Have your fishmonger remove the skin and gray fat underneath the skin of the salmon and buy a single piece if you can to make it easier to cut up.

  I like to serve this accompanied by crustless toast points.

Cut the salmon into ¼-inch slices across the grain. Dice finely.

Pinch the tops off the sprigs of chervil and save them to use as a garnish. Chop the remaining chervil.

Combine the salmon, chopped chervil, capers, lemon juice, salt and pepper in a large bowl. Taste and adjust the seasonings if necessary.

Cut the avocados in half lengthwise, remove the pits and scoop out the flesh. In a food processor, combine the onion, avocado, jalapeño, lime juice, cayenne, salt and pepper until smooth. Taste and adjust the seasonings if needed (it can afford to be a bit tart to counteract the richness of the salmon).

Spoon 2 Tbsp whipped avocado into each of four 1-cup wine glasses or straight-sided glasses. Follow with 3 Tbsp salmon and repeat the layers. Garnish each serving with a sprig of chervil and serve immediately.

BEAUTY TIP

Gourmet Gorgeous

You can make a nourishing mask that will leave your skin feeling moisturized by mashing half a small ripe avocado with a couple of teaspoons of yogurt and a few drops of honey. Smooth it on your face and relax for 15 minutes. Rinse with cold water.

Devin

CITRUS SHRIMP *with* GRAPEFRUIT, AVOCADO *and* RADISH

This salad is a cinch to pull together. I can buy precooked shrimp (you can even use frozen) at my local grocery store as well as all of the other simple-to-find ingredients.

You can present it as formally or as casually as you like. If you happen to own some ring molds, compose the salad by placing layers of the ingredients within the ring and removing it before drizzling with dressing for a tower-like effect.

This can be served as an elegant appetizer or in larger portions as a main course. To pull it together into a meal, try serving it with carrot gazpacho (page 71).

The dressing also makes a good topping for squid or salmon.

For the dressing, whisk together lime juice, oil, soy sauce, shallot, salt and pepper in a bowl. Set aside.

Using a sharp knife, slice the top and bottom off the grapefruit. Cut the rind and pith from the fruit from top to bottom. Remove each segment of fruit by slicing it away from the membranes.

Slice the radishes into very thin circles.

Cut the avocado in half lengthwise and remove the pit. Carefully peel off the skin and cut the avocado into slices ¼ inch thick. Sprinkle with the lime juice.

Very gently toss together the grapefruit, radishes, avocado, shrimp and dressing in a large bowl (be careful not to break apart the avocado). Divide the salad among 4 plates and top with a pinch of cayenne and 5 to 7 coriander leaves per plate.

SERVES 4

LIME SOY DRESSING
2 Tbsp freshly squeezed lime juice

1½ Tbsp vegetable oil

1 Tbsp soy sauce

1 Tbsp finely chopped shallot

½ tsp kosher salt

¼ tsp freshly ground black pepper

SALAD
2 pink grapefruit

3 radishes

1 large avocado

1 Tbsp freshly squeezed lime juice

12 large cooked shrimp, sliced in half lengthwise

⅛ tsp cayenne pepper

½ small bunch of fresh coriander

KITCHEN HINT

RIPENING AVOCADOS
To ripen avocados quickly, place them in a brown paper bag. The bag traps the ethylene gas that naturally escapes from the avocados and speeds up the ripening process. Scrunch the bag closed and the avocados should ripen in 1 to 3 days at room temperature. Adding an apple to the bag will increase the intensity of the ethylene and speed up the ripening even more.

Linda

3-lb (1.5 kg) cooked chicken

8 oz (250 g) asparagus, trimmed

1 Tbsp extra-virgin olive oil

1 Tbsp unsalted butter

10 oz (300 g) chanterelles
  or oyster mushrooms, cut in half
  or thirds if large

¼ tsp kosher salt

⅛ tsp freshly ground black pepper

1 small clove garlic, finely chopped

1 tsp freshly squeezed lemon juice

3 green onions, white and
  light-green parts only, sliced

1 Belgian endive (about 5 oz/150 g),
  cut in ¼-inch strips

15 cherry tomatoes, cut in half,
  or 3 medium heirloom tomatoes,
  seeded and cut in chunks

VINAIGRETTE

2 Tbsp balsamic vinegar

1 Tbsp red wine vinegar

2 tsp Dijon mustard

½ tsp kosher salt

3 Tbsp extra-virgin olive oil

¼ tsp freshly ground black pepper

WARM CHICKEN SALAD *with* ASPARAGUS, ENDIVE *and* SAUTÉED CHANTERELLES

I like to use Devin's roast chicken in this (page 146), but you can also roast four chicken breasts. If you use a storebought roast chicken, you will have this salad on the table in no time. A bit of chopping, a quick cooking of the asparagus and mushrooms and you're done.

Remove the chicken from the bones and tear it into bite-sized strips.

Bring a large skillet of salted water to a boil. Add the asparagus and cook for 3 to 5 minutes (depending on the thickness of the stalks), or until tender but still crisp. Immediately plunge into cold water to stop the cooking process and to retain the bright green color. Drain, pat dry and cut each spear diagonally into 3 pieces.

Heat the olive oil and butter in a large skillet over medium-high heat. Add the mushrooms and sauté for 4 minutes. Add the salt, pepper and garlic and sauté for 1 to 2 minutes, or until the mushrooms are cooked through. Stir in the lemon juice and cook for 30 seconds. Taste and adjust the seasonings, adding more lemon juice if needed.

Combine the chicken, asparagus, mushrooms, green onions, endive and tomatoes in a serving bowl.

For the vinaigrette, combine the vinegars, mustard and salt in a small bowl. After 5 minutes (this allows the salt to dissolve), whisk in the oil, then the pepper. Pour the vinaigrette over the salad and toss.

Devin

CRUNCHY PARMESAN MUSHROOMS ON ARUGULA

This warm mushroom salad is to die for. The mushrooms take 5 minutes to prepare and are light, salty, cheesy and crunchy all at the same time. The spicy arugula with a spray of lemon juice is the perfect pairing for the richer mushrooms. Using panko instead of regular breadcrumbs will make the mushrooms exceptionally light and crispy.

This can be served as a starter or as a main course with some good bread and an extra wedge of Parmesan cheese.

Preheat the broiler.

For the mushrooms, combine the Parmesan, breadcrumbs, salt and pepper in a shallow bowl.

Brush the olive oil over both sides of the mushrooms and dredge the mushrooms in the crumb mixture, pressing in the crumbs to make them stick.

Place the mushrooms on a greased baking sheet and sprinkle with the remaining crumbs. Place the baking sheet on the middle rack of the oven and broil for 5 minutes, or until the mushrooms are crispy and golden brown. Make sure to keep an eye on them, as they can burn easily.

Evenly divide the arugula among 4 plates and drizzle with the olive oil and lemon juice.

Arrange the mushrooms on the arugula and serve warm.

SERVES 4

PARMESAN MUSHROOMS
½ cup lightly packed grated
  Parmesan cheese

½ cup panko breadcrumbs

1 tsp kosher salt

¼ tsp freshly ground black pepper

¼ cup extra-virgin olive oil

10 oz (300 g) oyster mushrooms

SALAD
5 oz (150 g) arugula (4 to 5 cups
  lightly packed)

2 Tbsp extra-virgin olive oil

1½ Tbsp freshly squeezed lemon juice

. . . .
KITCHEN HINT

PANKO
Panko, or Japanese breadcrumbs, are made by coarsely grinding loaves of crustless white bread. The crumbs have the consistency of crushed cornflakes or potato chips. They have found a home in Western cooking due to their ability to absorb moisture while staying crisp and providing a crunchy texture with a neutral flavor.

. . . .

Linda

PROSCIUTTO *and* FIG BUNDLES
ON RICOTTA CROSTINI

When I'm in a French frame of mind, I turn to Devin's crunchy celery root salad (page 99), but if I want to conjure up memories of Tuscany, I make this, which includes two of my favorite Italian ingredients: prosciutto and smooth, slightly sweet ricotta cheese. Use a mild extra-virgin olive oil in the dressing (the Tuscan variety can be very piquant). If figs are out of season, you can substitute peeled peaches.

Toast the pine nuts in the oven at the same time as the figs. They should take about 3 to 5 minutes.

Preheat the oven to 375°F.

Cut a cross about ¾ inch deep in the top of each fig.

Form an X using 2 pieces of prosciutto. Place a fig at the intersection and drizzle 1 tsp port or port glaze over each fig. Wrap the prosciutto over the fig. Twist the excess prosciutto at the top and secure it with a toothpick. Place on a baking sheet and bake for 12 minutes, or until the meat is crisp and the figs are warmed through.

While the figs are baking, prepare the crostini by combining the ricotta and lemon zest in a small bowl.

Grill or toast the bread and spread ricotta on each slice. Sprinkle generously with salt and pepper.

For the salad, combine the mâche and chives in a bowl.

Whisk together the port, lemon juice and oil in a small bowl. Season with salt and pepper. Taste and adjust the seasonings, adding more lemon juice if needed. Add the vinaigrette to the lettuce and toss.

SERVES 4

FIGS

4 large fresh figs

8 large thin slices prosciutto

4 tsp ruby port or port glaze (page 98)

CROSTINI

½ cup ricotta cheese

1 tsp lightly packed grated lemon zest, preferably organic

4 slices baguette, about ¾ inch thick, cut on the diagonal

Kosher or sea salt and freshly ground black pepper to taste

SALAD

4 to 5 oz (125 to 150 g) mâche or mixed baby greens (about 4 cups lightly packed)

1 Tbsp lightly packed finely chopped fresh chives

1 tsp ruby port

2 tsp freshly squeezed lemon juice

2 Tbsp extra-virgin olive oil

Kosher salt and freshly ground black pepper to taste

¼ cup pine nuts, toasted

Divide the salad among 4 plates. Arrange the crostini and a fig on each plate. Sprinkle the pine nuts over top and serve while the crostini and figs are still warm.

PORT GLAZE

A delicious port glaze from super caterer and recipe tester, Jan Sherk. Drizzle it on fresh figs or pears or any blue cheese.

Combine ¼ cup port, 1 Tbsp honey and 5 black peppercorns in a small saucepan. Bring to a low boil and simmer for 5 minutes, or until syrupy. Cool and remove the peppercorns.

Makes about ¼ cup.

Devin

CELERY ROOT *and* APPLE SLAW
with SMOKED TROUT CROSTINI

SERVES 4 TO 6

This recipe is a jazzed-up version of celery root remoulade, which is a staple at any self-respecting bistro in France. Adding an apple brightens the flavor and makes it a perfect pairing for smoked trout. If you can't find smoked trout, smoked salmon is a great substitute. If you're feeling *molto* Italiano and *moyen* français, then Mom's prosciutto-wrapped figs (page 97) is the way to go.

Peel the celery root and roughly grate it into a large bowl of cold water with 2 Tbsp lemon juice to prevent browning. Set aside.

Peel, core and grate the apple and add it to the celery root.

In a separate large bowl, stir together the mayonnaise, onion, capers, salt, pepper and the remaining 2 Tbsp lemon juice.

Drain the celery root and apple, pressing out any excess water with the back of a large spoon. Wrap the celery root and apple in a tea towel and squeeze to dry as much as possible.

Add the celery root and apple to the mayonnaise mixture and gently stir to coat. Taste and add a little lemon juice if necessary.

Toast the slices of baguette and drizzle the olive oil evenly over the top. Top with pieces of smoked trout.

To serve, mound the celery root/apple mixture on a platter and surround with the crostini. Sprinkle with parsley.

1 celery root (about 1 lb/500 g)

¼ cup freshly squeezed lemon juice, divided

1 Granny Smith apple

⅓ cup mayonnaise

2 Tbsp finely chopped red onion

2 Tbsp capers

1 tsp kosher salt

¼ tsp freshly ground black pepper

6 slices baguette, ½ inch thick, cut on the diagonal

2 Tbsp extra-virgin olive oil

8 oz (250 g) boneless, skinless smoked trout (about 2 fillets), or 6 large slices smoked salmon, cut or broken in pieces

¼ cup lightly packed coarsely chopped fresh flat-leaf parsley

Comfort food never goes out of style. A delicious
meatloaf beats a badly cooked filet of beef any day.

LINDA

GOOD EATS FOR BAD DAYS

And good eats for good days, too! Sweet or savory,
these recipes need a chapter all on their own.

DEVIN

Linda

GRILLED GRUYÈRE, HAM *and* PEAR ON BAGUETTE

SERVES 4 TO 6

1 baguette, about 23 inches long

1 to 1½ Tbsp Dijon or honey mustard

8 to 10 thin slices Black Forest ham
(about 5 oz/150 g)

3 oz (90 g) Gruyère cheese,
thinly sliced

1 Bosc pear, unpeeled, cored and
sliced ¼ inch thick

When I'm in the mood for a comforting sandwich (which always means some form of melted cheese), it's hard to decide between Devin's Mona Lisa (page 104) and this fifteen-minute recipe. I like to use Black Forest ham, which is gently smoked, and good-quality Gruyère, which I usually have in my refrigerator.

Before you start to assemble this quick recipe, make sure your baguette can fit comfortably in your oven. Cut off the ends if necessary. It's important to wrap the sandwich in foil for the first 8 minutes of baking to melt the cheese and prevent the crust from becoming too hard, but you do want to open the foil for the last few minutes of baking so your sandwich has a crisp crust.

Preheat the oven to 400°F.

Cut the baguette in half lengthwise and spread the mustard over the bottom half.

Fold the ham slices in half and place the ham over the mustard, overlapping slightly as you go. Top with overlapping slices of cheese. Arrange the pear slices tightly over the cheese. (Eat any leftover pear.) Replace the top of the baguette.

Wrap the bread in foil and bake for 8 minutes. Open the foil and bake for another 5 minutes. Cut into 4 to 6 pieces and serve warm.

Devin

MONA LISA SANDWICH

SERVES 4

2 large boneless, skinless
  chicken breasts (about 6 to
  8 oz/175 to 250 g each)

½ cup dry breadcrumbs

1 tsp kosher salt

¼ tsp freshly ground black pepper

1 large egg white

½ cup mayonnaise

2 Tbsp pesto

5 oz (150 g) mozzarella cheese,
  sliced ⅛ inch thick

4 soft floured Portuguese rolls,
  cut in half

2 large tomatoes, sliced

12 whole fresh basil leaves

Sunny and Annie was the name of my corner deli when I lived in New York. The absolutely fantastic part about it was that they would deliver anything (even a pack of gum) to your apartment at any time of day or night. (Only in New York, right?) They made stellar sandwiches — probably forty varieties — all behind this tiny little counter by the cash register.

When my boyfriend came to visit me for the first time, we didn't really have much interest in leaving the apartment, so we called Sunny and asked her to deliver two Mona Lisas — the house specialty. What arrived was the best deli sandwich I have ever tasted. Warm crispy breaded chicken on a Portuguese bun with melting mozzarella, tomato and pesto mayonnaise.

This is my best attempt to reproduce the sandwich of all sandwiches.

Preheat the oven to 400°F.

Cut each chicken breast in half lengthwise and lightly pound to flatten slightly.

In a shallow bowl, mix together the breadcrumbs, salt and pepper. In another shallow bowl, lightly whisk the egg white.

Dip each chicken piece into the egg white and then into the breadcrumb mixture, pressing the crumbs onto all sides. Place on a greased baking sheet and bake for 12 minutes.

While the chicken is in the oven, combine the mayonnaise and pesto in a small bowl.

Turn the chicken and top with the cheese. Put the rolls in the oven to toast and return the chicken to the oven to cook for 3 to 4 more minutes, or until the cheese has melted.

Spread mayonnaise on the bottom half of each roll. Top with the chicken, tomato, basil and the top half of the roll. Serve warm.

KITCHEN HINTS

DRY BREADCRUMBS

If you wish, cut the crusts off a loaf of stale bread. If the bread is very, very dry, break it in pieces, place the pieces in a food processor fitted with the steel blade and process until the crumbs are the consistency of grainy sand.

If the bread is not completely dry, tear it into ½-inch pieces and spread on a baking sheet. Toast in a 325°F oven until a piece crumbles between your fingers; timing will depend on the freshness of the bread. Reduce the heat if the bread gets too dark. Process as above.

Freeze the breadcrumbs in a plastic bag for up to 6 months.

Makes about 2 cups.

FRESH BREADCRUMBS

Remove the crust from a loaf of bread (no more than a day old; it should not be bone dry). Tear the bread into ½-inch pieces. Place in a food processor fitted with the steel blade and process until the bread is in pieces (⅛ inch or smaller). Don't overprocess or you may end up with a ball of gummy bread.

For fine crumbs, spread the crumbs on a baking sheet and let them air-dry a bit, then force them through a sieve.

The fresh breadcrumbs can be frozen in a plastic bag for up to 6 months.

Makes about 4¾ cups.

Linda

CAPRESE PASTA

40 to 45 cherry tomatoes, cut in half
   and seeded, or 8 medium tomatoes,
   seeded and coarsely chopped

½ tsp kosher salt

1 lb (500 g) penne

¼ cup extra-virgin olive oil

2 large cloves garlic, grated

5 to 6 bocconcini (about 2 inches in
   diameter), cut in ¼-inch dice

8 leaves fresh basil, shredded

1½ oz (45 g) baby arugula
   (about 1½ cups lightly packed)

Sea salt and coarsely ground
   black pepper to taste

A Caprese salad is traditionally composed of tomatoes, bocconcini and basil, replicating the colors of the Italian flag. My take on that theme is a sauce that can be ready in the time it takes to boil your pasta. I first tasted a version of this at my friend Harriet's beautiful century-old cottage on Sturgeon Lake, but like other wonderful recipes, it has many mothers. Harriet claims she learned it from our mutual friend Paola, and it is now a summer standby in our house. Every member of the family has a different take. Devin puts in few extra handfuls of basil and uses different-colored tomatoes, while my son, Luke, ramps up the arugula and sometimes adds black olives and diced cooked bacon or prosciutto.

Place the tomatoes in a large serving bowl and sprinkle with the kosher salt (this can be done up to 2 hours ahead).

Bring a large pot of salted water to a boil. Add the penne and cook until *al dente*.

Combine the oil and garlic in a small cold skillet. Cook over medium heat, stirring often (the oil should be gently foaming), until the garlic is barely colored, about 1 to 1½ minutes. You don't want the garlic to burn. Immediately pour the hot oil and garlic over the tomatoes and toss.

Drain the penne. Add it to the tomatoes with the bocconcini, basil, arugula, sea salt and pepper and toss. Serve immediately.

Devin

PENNE *with* PEAS *and* SAGE

Simple, fresh, fast and delicious. I mean, how easy is it just to boil up some pasta, grab some frozen peas and lightly fry some fresh sage? This is one of my favorite last-minute dinners when I've forgotten to go grocery shopping. Don't be alarmed at what may seem to be too much cream. Just let it sit for 5 minutes and the pasta will soak it all up (this is when I usually set the table!), leaving it smooth and creamy.

Bring a large pot of salted water to a boil. Add the pasta and cook until almost *al dente*. Add the peas and continue to cook until the peas are hot and the pasta is *al dente*.

Meanwhile, heat the oil in a large skillet over medium-high heat. Add the sage leaves in a single layer, being careful not to overlap. Fry for 1 minute. Turn and cook for another minute, or until the sage begins to brown and become crisp. Remove the sage and drain on a paper towel.

Drain the pasta and peas.

Place the cream, garlic, salt and pepper in the pasta pot over medium heat and bring to a simmer for a minute or so.

Return the pasta and peas to the pasta pot. Stir in ½ cup Parmesan.

Transfer to a large serving bowl and allow the pasta to sit for 5 minutes. Give the pasta a few more tosses and top with the fried sage leaves and the remaining Parmesan.

SERVES 4 TO 6

1 lb (500 g) penne

2½ cups frozen baby peas

2 Tbsp olive oil

15 to 20 fresh sage leaves

2 cups 35% (whipping) cream

1 large clove garlic, grated

1½ tsp kosher salt

¼ tsp freshly ground black pepper

¾ cup lightly packed grated Parmesan cheese, divided

Linda

ASIAN GLAZED MEATLOAF

ASIAN GLAZE

1 Tbsp vegetable oil

3 large cloves garlic, grated

2 tsp grated gingerroot

5 green onions, white and light-green parts only, finely chopped

⅔ cup soy sauce

⅔ cup liquid honey

¾ tsp sesame oil

MEATLOAF

2 tsp vegetable oil

4 cups finely diced white or cremini mushrooms (about 12 oz/375 g)

3 green onions, white and light-green parts only, finely chopped

1 large clove garlic, grated

Pinch of kosher salt

3 Tbsp rice wine

2 Tbsp water

1 lb (500 g) minced pork

1 lb (500 g) minced beef, preferably sirloin

¼ cup unreduced Asian Glaze

1 large egg, lightly beaten

½ cup silken tofu

¾ cup fresh breadcrumbs (page 105)

½ tsp kosher salt

¼ tsp freshly ground black pepper

I have to admit that my son, Luke, is the creative spark behind this recipe. He's the guy who came up with the tantalizing glaze. The addition of sautéed mushrooms and silken tofu make for a moist and tender texture. I suspect most of you have a favorite meatloaf recipe that is brushed with chili sauce or ketchup. This is for the days when you are prepared to do a little switch-up.

I like to serve it with stir-fried sugar snaps and creamy mashed potatoes. It's also great the next day on a crusty white roll spread with Dijon or English mustard, some sliced cucumber, lettuce and — okay — a tomato.

For the glaze, heat the oil, garlic, ginger and green onions in a small saucepan over medium heat. Cook, stirring, for about 1 minute, or until the onions are soft but not browned. Add the soy sauce, honey and sesame oil and stir until the honey melts. Set aside ½ cup for the meatloaf and glazing.

Increase the heat to high and cook the remaining glaze for a couple of minutes, or until the liquid has reduced to about ⅔ cup. Set aside for your drizzle — do not use this in the meatloaf.

Preheat the oven to 375°F.

For the meatloaf, heat the oil in a large skillet over medium heat. Add the mushrooms and green onions and sauté until the vegetables are soft but not browned, about 5 minutes.

Add the garlic and a pinch of salt. Stir and cook for about a minute. Pour in the rice wine and water and stir until the liquid has reduced to 2 Tbsp. Remove from the heat and transfer to a bowl to cool slightly.

In a large bowl, combine the pork, beef, mushroom mixture, ¼ cup unreduced glaze, egg, tofu, breadcrumbs, salt and pepper. Mix together with your hands until all the ingredients are combined.

Place a wire rack on a baking sheet. Lay a piece of foil over the rack and pierce it in several places with a fork. This will allow the fat from the meatloaf to run onto the baking sheet, leaving the sides of the loaf well browned and crisp.

Form the meat into a log shape with blunt ends and brush with the unreduced glaze. You will be brushing the meat two or three more times.

Bake the meatloaf for 60 to 70 minutes, basting once or twice with unreduced glaze. The meatloaf is ready when the juices are pale golden when the loaf is pierced with a skewer, and the internal temperature reaches 160°F (71°C).

Transfer the meatloaf to a cutting board and let rest for 10 minutes to allow the juices to disperse throughout the meatloaf before slicing. To serve, slice and drizzle with the reduced Asian glaze.

Devin

SERVES 6

2 large sweet potatoes
(about 1½ lbs/750 g total), peeled
and cut in 2-inch chunks

2 baking potatoes
(about 1½ lbs/750 g total), peeled
and cut in 1-inch chunks

1 clove garlic, peeled

2 Tbsp extra-virgin olive oil, divided

1 cup coarsely chopped cooking onion
(about 1 medium)

3 cloves garlic, finely chopped

¾ cup diced carrot

2 stalks celery, diced

1 cup frozen peas

2½ lbs (1.25 kg) ground turkey

1 tsp grated gingerroot

2 tsp kosher salt, divided

½ tsp cayenne, divided

½ tsp ground cumin

¼ tsp ground cinnamon

1 Tbsp all-purpose flour

¾ cup skim milk, warm

½ cup low-fat yogurt,
at room temperature

TURKEY SHEPHERD'S PIE
with SWEET POTATO CRUST

You might think that the words "comfort food" and "healthy" don't belong in the same recipe, but here they certainly do. I am such a sucker for shepherd's pie, but sometimes find that its heavy richness can be a bit much — at least after my third serving. So this recipe uses ground turkey, skim milk and low-fat yogurt, reducing the fat but none of the flavor. The sweet potato crust is a great alternative to your typical white potato and really adds a punch when perked up with cayenne pepper and cinnamon.

Place the sweet potatoes, potatoes and whole garlic clove in a large pot of salted water. Bring to a boil and cook for 12 to 15 minutes, or until tender. Drain, return to the pot and set aside.

While the potatoes are cooking, heat 1 Tbsp oil in a large, deep skillet over medium-high heat. Add the onion and sauté for 5 to 6 minutes, or until transparent and soft.

Add the chopped garlic, carrot and celery. Reduce the heat to medium and sauté for 5 minutes.

Stir in the peas and cook for 1 minute.

Remove the vegetables from the skillet, transfer to a small bowl and set aside. Wipe the skillet clean with a paper towel and return to medium-high heat. Heat the remaining 1 Tbsp oil.

Add the ground turkey, ginger, 1 tsp salt, ¼ tsp cayenne, cumin and cinnamon and cook, stirring, for 5 minutes.

Sprinkle on the flour and cook, stirring, for 2 minutes, or until the turkey is cooked through and the juices have thickened.

Return the vegetables to the skillet, combine with the turkey and remove the pan from the heat.

Preheat the oven to 400°F.

Place the pot of drained potatoes over low heat. Add the warm milk, yogurt, the remaining ½ tsp salt and ¼ tsp cayenne. Mash together with a hand masher or hand-held mixer.

Spoon the turkey mixture into a 13- by 9-inch baking dish. Spread the potato mixture on top in an even layer.

Bake for 20 minutes, or until the top is golden brown.

. . . .

KITCHEN HINT

GINGERROOT

Ginger is an important ingredient in many traditional Chinese medicines. It is used to treat headaches, aid digestion and combat nausea. Store it in the vegetable drawer of your refrigerator or freeze it, tightly wrapped.

To remove the peel, try scraping the edge of a spoon along the skin of the root. If the skin is tough, use a knife.

. . . .

GINGER TEA FOR TWO

After a day of writing and testing recipes, Mom and I will sit down for a cup of fresh ginger tea. We put a couple of tablespoons of finely chopped gingerroot in a tea ball or sieve of a Japanese tea pot and pour 2 to 3 cups of boiling water over it. Then we let it steep for about 4 minutes. It's a guaranteed antidote for overeating. If I have a sore throat, I make a weaker brew and add a little honey.

Linda

SOFT POLENTA *with* CHICKEN, MUSHROOMS *and* CAPERS

I love Devin's quick mac and cheese (page 117), but when I have a little more time and energy I like to make this very comforting dish for a casual weekend dinner. All the components except the polenta can be made ahead and reheated, or you could open a bottle of wine, invite everyone into the kitchen and have them help you get this one-dish wonder to the table.

Polenta, a northern Italian staple, is usually made with yellow cornmeal, although the Venetians sometimes prefer the more delicate white cornmeal. I use the traditional long-cooking method, although some cooks bake it in the oven or use the instant polenta that is ready in a few minutes. Although you may have eaten cooled and grilled polenta in Italian restaurants, this recipe calls for the polenta to be creamy and the consistency of porridge.

For the polenta, bring the stock and milk to a low boil in a large saucepan. Add the salt and quickly whisk in the cornmeal. Reduce the heat to medium and cook for about 30 minutes, stirring often, until the polenta pulls away from the sides of the pan. Stir in the cheese. The polenta will thicken if it is not served immediately. Stir in ½ cup warm milk before plating if necessary.

While the polenta is cooking, sprinkle the chicken strips with salt and pepper.

Heat the oil in a large skillet over high heat. Add the chicken and sauté for 4 to 5 minutes, or until cooked through. Remove the chicken to a plate.

Add the wine, orange juice and lemon juice to the skillet and cook, stirring, for 1 to 2 minutes, or until the liquid has reduced by half. Stir in the capers. Remove from the pan and add to the chicken.

For the mushrooms, heat the oil in the same skillet used to

SERVES 4

POLENTA

2 cups chicken stock

2 cups whole milk

¼ tsp kosher salt

½ cup fine or medium cornmeal

¼ cup lightly packed finely grated Parmesan cheese (about ¾ oz/20 g)

½ cup warm whole milk, optional

CHICKEN

1 lb (500 g) chicken scaloppine or boneless, skinless chicken breast, pounded thin and cut in 1-inch strips

½ tsp kosher salt

¼ tsp freshly ground black pepper

1½ Tbsp olive oil

¼ cup dry white wine

2 Tbsp freshly squeezed orange juice

2 Tbsp freshly squeezed lemon juice

2 Tbsp capers

MUSHROOMS

1 Tbsp olive oil

8 oz (250 g) white or cremini
  mushrooms, sliced ¼ inch thick

1 Tbsp finely chopped cooking onion

1 clove garlic, finely chopped

1 tsp lightly packed finely chopped
  fresh rosemary

Pinch of kosher salt

1 Tbsp unsalted butter

½ cup dry white wine

14-oz (398 mL) can diced tomatoes,
  loosely drained

2 Tbsp lightly packed finely chopped
  fresh parsley

Sprigs of fresh rosemary, for garnish

cook the chicken. Add the mushrooms, reduce the heat to medium and cook for about 5 minutes, or until the mushrooms have released their liquid.

Add the onion, garlic, rosemary, salt and butter and sauté for about 10 minutes, or until the pan is dry and the mushrooms are golden brown around the edges.

Pour in the wine, raise the heat to high and cook for a few minutes, or until the liquid has reduced by half. Add the drained tomatoes, reduce the heat and simmer for 5 minutes.

Return the chicken to the skillet and cook for 2 to 3 minutes to heat through. Taste and adjust the seasonings if necessary.

Spoon the polenta into a heated serving dish or individual shallow bowls. Top with mushrooms and chicken. Sprinkle with parsley and decorate with rosemary sprigs. Serve immediately.

. . . .

KITCHEN HINT

CHICKEN SCALOPPINE

To flatten chicken for scaloppine, lay a boneless, skinless chicken breast on a cutting board. Slice through just over three-quarters of the way along the long side of the breast and open the flap like a book.

Place the open breast on a piece of waxed paper or parchment paper. Cover with another piece of paper. Pound the meat with a rolling pin or empty beer or wine bottle until the breasts are about ¼ to ⅓ inch thick.

. . . .

Devin

LEMON *and* PARMESAN ORZO MAC *and* CHEESE *with* CHICKEN MEATBALLS

Let me explain why this recipe just had to be in this book. I feel I owe it to you and the world at large to proclaim this as the ultimate cure for a late night out with one too many drinks. Which means, yes, I have had this for breakfast. It also doubles as the most comforting meal after a terrible day at work. I don't know what the science is behind it all, but it instantly puts all wrongs to right.

If you don't have the energy to make the meatballs, the orzo is still amazing on its own. The Parmesan and butter create a creamy and comforting sauce and the lemon and chives just give it an extra punch of flavor. Baking the meatballs instead of frying them not only reduces the washing-up time; it also keeps the meatballs soft and tender. (Perfect for when chewing itself feels like work!)

I've been known to eat this right out of the pot, but if you are serving it to guests, you can top each bowl with an extra grating of Parmesan and a few whole chives.

Preheat the oven to 450°F.

In a large bowl, combine the chicken, breadcrumbs, egg, garlic, salt and pepper. Form the mixture into 12 balls about 1½ inches in diameter. Place on a parchment-lined baking sheet and bake for 20 minutes, or until golden and cooked through.

While the meatballs are in the oven, bring a large pot of salted water to a boil. Add the orzo and cook according to the package directions.

Drain the orzo and return it to the pot. Stir in the butter, salt and pepper. Add the Parmesan, chives and lemon zest and mix until combined.

Evenly divide the orzo among 4 serving bowls and top each serving with 3 meatballs.

SERVES 4

CHICKEN MEATBALLS

1½ lbs (750 g) ground chicken breast (not extra lean)

⅓ cup dry breadcrumbs (page 105)

1 large egg

3 cloves garlic, grated

1 tsp kosher salt

¼ tsp freshly ground black pepper

ORZO

2 cups orzo

3 Tbsp unsalted butter

1 tsp kosher salt

¼ tsp freshly ground black pepper

1 cup lightly packed finely grated Parmesan cheese (about 3 oz/90 g)

1 Tbsp lightly packed chopped fresh chives

1 Tbsp lightly packed grated lemon zest (about 1 medium), preferably organic

Linda

SERVES 2

2 Tbsp unsalted butter, divided

2 thick slices crustless Calabrese,
   sourdough or other dense white
   bread or focaccia, cut in
   ½-inch cubes (about 1½ cups)

Heaping ⅛ tsp cayenne pepper

4 large eggs, poached (page 22)

½ cup whole milk yogurt,
   at room temperature

Kosher or sea salt and freshly ground
   black pepper to taste

SPICED TURKISH POACHED
EGGS *with* YOGURT

I first had these unusual poached eggs when my husband, Martin, and I visited Istanbul a few years ago. Called *cilbir*, they were one of the few true Turkish items on the breakfast menu at our hotel. They quickly became my morning staple, and when we came home I decided to replicate them for the family. The only change to an otherwise very traditional recipe is the addition of croutons.

Melt 1 Tbsp butter in a large skillet over medium-high heat. Add the bread cubes and sauté for 4 to 5 minutes, or until golden brown. Divide between two deep bowls large enough to hold 2 eggs each.

Melt the remaining 1 Tbsp butter in a small saucepan, add the cayenne and keep warm.

Place the poached eggs over the croutons. Top with yogurt, drizzle with cayenne butter and sprinkle with salt and pepper. Eat immediately.

BEAUTY TIP

Yogurt on Your Face

Although yogurt is an excellent source of calcium and phosphorus, it can also be incorporated into a wonderful mask for oily skin.

   Mix 1½ Tbsp rolled oats into ¼ cup whole-milk yogurt (bring the yogurt to room temperature before using, otherwise this mask is really cold!). Add 5 drops freshly squeezed lime or lemon juice. Pat onto your face and relax for 10 to 15 minutes. Wash off with warm water and follow with your favorite toner and cream.

Devin

COMFORTING EGG DROP PARMESAN SOUP

This soup serves me very well when I'm feeling under the weather. It's easy on the tummy and nourishing. Adding the cornstarch to the raw egg makes the egg incredible silky and light by stabilizing the liquid proteins when they are heated, so there's no shrinkage and no rubbery texture.

I eat this with lots of crusty bread. Mom sometimes adds a cooked and shredded chicken breast.

Bring the chicken stock to a boil in a large pot.

Mix the cornstarch and water in a small jug or measuring cup. Add the egg to the cornstarch and water and beat with a fork until well incorporated.

Remove the stock from the heat. Without stirring the soup, slowly drizzle very thin streams of the egg mixture in a circular motion. Let the soup sit for 1 minute.

Return the pot to medium-high heat and bring the soup to a simmer. Immediately remove the pot from the heat and add the parsley, chives, thyme, pepper and lemon zest. Use the bottom of a ladle to break up any large pieces of egg.

Serve immediately sprinkled with Parmesan.

SERVES 4

4 cups chicken stock

½ tsp cornstarch

1 tsp water

1 large egg

1 Tbsp lightly packed finely chopped fresh parsley

1 Tbsp lightly packed finely chopped fresh chives

½ tsp lightly packed finely chopped fresh thyme

¼ tsp freshly ground black pepper

1 tsp lightly packed grated lemon zest, preferably organic

½ cup lightly packed grated Parmesan cheese (about 1½ oz/45 g)

Linda

FONDUTA

2 large egg yolks

¼ cup whole milk

8 oz (250 g) Italian Fontina cheese,
    cut in ¼-inch dice

1 Tbsp unsalted butter, cold

¼ cup dry white wine

4 to 6 slices Calabrese, baguette
    or dense white bread, about
    ¾ inch thick

Coarsely ground black pepper to taste

1 white truffle, optional

Fonduta is the ultimate comfort food – rich runny cheese bound with egg yolk and a little wine, poured over thick grilled bread. I think of it as the Italian version of a grilled cheese sandwich. A northern dish, mentioned in eighteenth-century Italian cookbooks, it is made with Fontina, a medium-bodied buttery cheese that varies in color from straw-white to deep yellow, depending on the season. Try to get the authentic Italian version when making this dish; some of the "imposters" are very salty.

Although the Italians serve this as an appetizer or quick snack, it makes a low-key light lunch or supper with a green salad and a glass of wine.

Whisk the egg yolks and milk in the top of a double boiler. Add the cheese and butter. Place over simmering water, making sure the bottom of the bowl holding the ingredients doesn't touch the hot water. Stir continuously until the cheese has melted and the ingredients have come together, about 6 minutes.

Slowly whisk in the wine and continue to cook, whisking every 20 seconds or so, for 5 minutes. The mixture should thicken slightly.

Meanwhile, grill or toast the bread. Place the bread on individual serving plates and pour the fonduta over each slice. Generously top with black pepper and a few shavings of truffle if you wish.

Devin

GOOEY MINI CAKES
FOR CHOCOLATE ADDICTS

Mom prefers gooey cheese as her comfort food; I, on the other hand, will always choose gooey melted chocolate.

It is vital that you beat the eggs until they reach the "ribbon" stage. The air that is beaten into the eggs supports the cakes' structure once the heavier chocolate and flour are added.

Melt the chocolate and butter in a bowl over a pot of simmering water, stirring constantly, making sure the bottom of the bowl does not touch the water. Once melted, remove from the heat and stir in the vanilla. Set aside.

In a separate bowl, whisk together the flour, baking powder, salt and cinnamon.

Using a mixer set on high, beat the eggs, egg yolks and sugar in a large bowl until the mixture turns pale yellow and "ribbons" fall when the beaters are lifted (this will take some time, but it's an important step).

Sift the flour mixture over the egg batter and then gently fold in until all the flour streaks have disappeared. Fold in the chocolate mixture until incorporated.

Transfer the batter to eight 1-cup ramekins (fill until about three-quarters full). Wrap the ramekins tightly with plastic wrap and freeze if you are not baking them right away.

Preheat the oven to 400°F.

Place the ramekins on a baking sheet and bake on the bottom rack for 10 to 12 minutes, or until the top is cracked but the middle is still slightly wobbly. (A skewer should pick up some moist crumbs when removed. If there are still traces of liquid chocolate, bake for 1 to 2 minutes longer.) Let sit for up to 5 minutes before eating.

SERVES 8

7 oz (210 g) semisweet chocolate, coarsely chopped

1 cup unsalted butter, at room temperature

½ tsp vanilla extract

½ cup all-purpose flour

¼ tsp baking powder

¼ tsp kosher salt

⅛ tsp ground cinnamon

4 large eggs

3 large egg yolks

¾ cup granulated sugar

KITCHEN HINT

BAKING FROZEN CAKES
The uncooked batter can be frozen in the ramekins. To bake, remove the plastic wrap and place the frozen ramekins on a baking sheet. Bake on the bottom rack of a 400°F oven for 20 to 24 minutes. Place a sheet of foil over the cakes after 15 minutes if the tops are browning.

Linda

SERVES 6 (PLUS A LITTLE
LEFTOVER FOR THE COOK)

PLUM COULIS

2½ lbs (1 kg) Angelino plums, pitted
    and cut in ½-inch slices

⅓ cup water

½ cup granulated sugar

1 vanilla bean, split lengthwise,
    or 1 tsp vanilla extract

⅛ tsp ground nutmeg

TAPIOCA PUDDING

⅓ cup small tapioca pearls

2½ cups whole milk, divided

1 cup coconut milk

2 Tbsp granulated sugar

Pinch of kosher salt

1 vanilla bean, split lengthwise,
    or 2 tsp vanilla extract

1 large egg, separated

COCONUT TAPIOCA PUDDING
with PLUM COULIS

My mom was the rice pudding aficionado in my family (see page 124), and Dad was a big fan of tapioca. This is a glammed-up version — elegant enough for a dinner party — of the tapioca pudding Mom used to make for him. If you're not a coconut fan, use more whole milk. If you can't find Angelinos, use any purple plums.

You may have extra plum coulis, but it should keep in the refrigerator for at least three weeks. Try it over frozen yogurt (page 209) or pound cake (page 208).

For the plum coulis, combine the plums and water in a large heavy saucepan over medium-low heat. Cook for 20 to 30 minutes, or until the fruit has softened. Stir frequently, mashing the plums with a wooden spoon or potato masher.

Push the fruit through a sieve or food mill, extracting as much of the juice and flesh as possible. You should have about 3 cups. If you are using a sieve, this will take some time. (When Devin makes this she skips this step and just throws the whole thing into a food processor, skins and all.)

Return the puree to the saucepan. Add the sugar, vanilla bean and nutmeg. Cook over medium heat and stir until the sugar has completely dissolved (do not let it boil, but tiny bubbles will appear). Taste, and if the plums are very sour, you may want to add a touch more sugar. Stirring occasionally, continue to simmer for about 30 minutes, or until the mixture has thickened and pulls away from the bottom of the pan when stirred. Let cool and remove the vanilla bean. Scrape the seeds from the bean into the coulis and stir in.

For the pudding, combine the tapioca and ½ cup milk in a saucepan and let soak for 30 minutes.

Stir in the remaining 2 cups milk, coconut milk, sugar, salt and

KITCHEN HINT

TAPIOCA

Tapioca is a flavorless, odorless, colorless starch extracted from the root of the cassava plant, and it is primarily used as a thickening agent. It comes in various forms — flakes, coarse meal, sticks and pearls of varying sizes. Pearl tapioca is used in puddings and in bubble tea.

Instant tapioca can be used to thicken fruit pie fillings; it gives fillings a glossy sheen and can be cooked for long periods of time.

vanilla bean. Bring to a low boil and simmer, stirring often, until the tapioca is translucent and cooked through, about 25 to 35 minutes. (Larger tapioca pearls will take longer to cook through.) Remove the pan from the heat and remove the vanilla bean. Scrape out the seeds and stir them into the tapioca.

Whisk the egg yolk in a small bowl. Stir in ¼ cup hot tapioca to temper the egg. Whisk all the egg into the tapioca and return to the heat. Cook for 30 seconds, whisking constantly. Transfer the tapioca to a large bowl. Chill by setting the bowl in a larger bowl of ice.

When the pudding is cool, beat the egg white in a separate bowl until it holds soft peaks. Gently fold the white thoroughly into the pudding.

To assemble, spoon 2 Tbsp plum coulis into each of four ¾-cup glasses. Add ¼ cup tapioca followed by another 2 Tbsp coulis and a final ¼ cup tapioca. Finish with a dollop of coulis.

5½ cups whole milk

3 Tbsp maple syrup

1 tsp vanilla extract

1 tsp lightly packed grated lemon zest, preferably organic

2 Tbsp unsalted butter

1 cup Arborio rice

1 cup raisins

¼ tsp ground cinnamon

NANA'S HEAVENLY RICE PUDDING

The simple pleasure of rice pudding is not to be taken lightly. Nothing gives you such pure instant comfort. My nana always said that her idea of perfect happiness would be sitting on a cloud while little angels fed this to her with a golden spoon. Anyway, give it a go and you'll be transported — maybe not to a cloud, but to some place very, very good.

The rice pudding can be stored in the refrigerator for up to five days. When reheating, add ¼ to ½ cup milk to return it to the original consistency.

Use Arborio (risotto) rice in this. You'll end up with a much creamier pudding because of the higher starch content.

In a small saucepan, bring the milk, maple syrup, vanilla and lemon zest to a simmer over medium heat.

In a separate large saucepan, melt the butter over medium-high heat. Add the rice and raisins and stir for 2 to 3 minutes, or until slightly toasted.

Pour the warmed milk mixture over the rice and raisins. Give it a few stirs and bring to a low simmer. Cook with the lid slightly ajar for 20 to 25 minutes, or until the rice is tender (taste it). Be sure to stir every 5 to 10 minutes.

Remove from the heat and add the cinnamon. Serve warm.

NANA'S BEAUTY TIPS

My nana loved to come up with homemade beauty treatments. They were a fun and inexpensive way for her to pamper herself and others.

These are two of my favorites:

Better Than Botox

I love using this mask before I put on my makeup. It tightens the pores and absorbs excess oil.

Squeeze half a lemon into a lightly beaten egg white. Apply to your face and neck and leave on for 30 minutes. Rinse with warm water.

Makes enough for two faces.

Energy Mask

This excellent skin brightener will revive any dull winter complexion. The mask is a little goopy, but it really leaves your skin glowing.

Combine 1 egg white, 1 tsp lemon juice, 1 tsp honey, ½ cup mashed strawberries and 1½ Tbsp minced fresh mint leaves in a small bowl. Mix together and apply for 10 minutes. Rinse and follow with your favorite moisturizer.

Makes enough for two faces.

Linda

4 ripe passionfruit

. . . .

KITCHEN HINT

PASSIONFRUIT

Dark purple passionfruit, no bigger than a small lemon, has a fresh, tangy taste with a hint of sweetness. The fruit has a shiny skin that becomes brittle and wrinkled when ripe. Its orange-yellow pulp, containing dark seeds, is traditionally used in desserts, sorbets, custards and jam, or is juiced for cocktails or soft drinks.

. . . .

LUKE'S ICED PASSIONFRUIT

When my son, Luke, worked in Uganda, he lived in the town of Mbarara. Ice cream, a favorite food of his, was hard to find, so he would take home a few passionfruit and stick them in the freezer for an hour. The result was a frozen delight, sweet and tart at the same time. If you leave the fruit in the freezer for too long the fruit will be too hard to enjoy. Just leave it on the counter for about 30 minutes before digging in. I promise you that this will become a fast-food favorite in your house.

Pop the passionfruit into the freezer for 1½ hours. Cut it in half with a saw-toothed knife and scoop out the flesh with a spoon. Fantastic!

Devin

CHOCOLATE BUTTER

MAKES ABOUT 1½ CUPS

This recipe contains the same ingredients as chocolate ganache or beautiful rich truffles. For the ratio of chocolate and cream that I use, the result is a creamy, thick and spreadable chocolate "butter." I love the idea of just pulling this out of my fridge whenever I like to put on a piece of fruit, sandwich between butter cookies or even spread on warm toast when I feel like a special treat. Mom also uses this recipe in her chocolate tarts (page 178). The chocolate butter melts when it is baked and makes a gooey warm filling.

1 cup 35% (whipping) cream

6 oz (175 g) semisweet chocolate, finely chopped (about 1 cup)

½ tsp vanilla extract

Pinch of kosher salt

Over low heat, bring the cream to a simmer in a heavy saucepan.

Add the chocolate, vanilla and salt. Stir continuously until the chocolate melts and the mixture is smooth and has lost its graininess. Do not let the mixture come to a boil.

Cool and refrigerate for at least 2 hours before using (the final consistency should be the same as room temperature butter).

LAVENDER LEMON TISANE

I make this "magic tea" with my little niece—it's a pretty impressive trick if there are kids around. Dried lavender buds are available in most health food stores.

Place 1½ tsp organic or tea-grade dried lavender buds in the strainer of a tea pot or in a tea ball inside a tea pot. Heat water to just below boiling, or bring to a boil and then remove from the heat for 30 seconds. Pour 4 cups water into the pot. Steep for 3 to 5 minutes.

Pour the tea into cups (this looks especially pretty in glass cups) and squeeze 3 or 4 drops of lemon juice into each cup. The pale mauve tea will turn a lovely pink.

Serves 4.

My favorite meal to prepare – dinner. What other task allows you to have a glass of wine on the job?

LINDA

TIME FOR DINNER

I'm not above ordering take-out after a hard day, but I do love the ritual of cooking dinner. It's my way to relax.

DEVIN

Mains

Pan-seared Salmon on Herbed Vegetables with Lemon Mustard Drizzle	130	Honey-roasted Halibut on Soba Noodles with Bok Choy and Mushrooms	132
Grilled Arctic Char with Lime-scented Watermelon and Cucumber Salad	134	Five-minute Asian Grilled Squid	135
Scallops with Leek and Morel Ragout	137	Grilled Shrimp with Charred Radicchio, Fingerlings and Aïoli	138
Moroccan-spiced Cornish Hens with Roasted Oranges, Onions and Figs	140	Sesame Chicken with Mango, Green Onion and Ginger Salsa	143
Roasted Duck Breast with Dried Cherry Shallot Compote	144	Roast Chicken with Prosciutto-wrapped Apricot Kebabs	146
Veal Chops on Roasted Apples and Vegetables with Herbed Bacon Vinaigrette	148	Sweet and Sticky Pork Chops with Glazed Dates	150
Butterflied Leg of Lamb with Grilled Nectarine and Onion Chutney	152	Argentinian Flank Steak with Caramelized Onions and Chimichurri	154
Aix-en-Provence Black Olive Tart	157	Three-Cheese Puff Pastry Tart	159

Sides

Cauliflower with Brown Butter, Pine Nuts and Lemon	160	Charred Broccoli with Spiced Yogurt	161
Corn Toss	162	Husk-on Roasted Corn with Chipotle Lime Butter	163
Slow-cooked Red Cabbage with Sweet Apple	164	Shredded Brussels Sprouts with Cranberries, Pecans and Shallots	165
Provençal Tomato, Onion and Zucchini Gratin	166	Zucchini Ribbons with Toasted Garlic Anchovy Breadcrumbs	169
Jerusalem Artichoke, Onion and Celery Root Gratin with Parmesan Crust	170	Apple and Cheddar Scalloped Potatoes	171
Sweet Butter Caramelized Carrots with Marsala Glaze	172	Sweet Potato, Spinach and Goat Cheese Gratin	175

Linda

PAN-SEARED SALMON ON HERBED VEGETABLES *with* LEMON MUSTARD DRIZZLE

SERVES 6

LEMON MUSTARD DRIZZLE

1½ Tbsp grainy mustard

2 Tbsp freshly squeezed lemon juice
 (about ½ medium)

¼ tsp kosher salt

¼ cup extra-virgin olive oil

1 clove garlic, peeled and
 lightly crushed

⅛ tsp freshly ground black pepper

SALMON

6 7-oz (200 g) salmon fillets, organic
 or wild if possible, skin removed

2 Tbsp extra-virgin olive oil

1 tsp kosher salt

½ tsp freshly ground black pepper

I first made this dish at our house in the country for my stepson Johnny, his wife, Shauna, and their toddler twins. I'd bought vegetables at a local roadside stand at the tail end of the asparagus season, when small green beans were just making their way into the market. The beets provide a flavor and texture contrast (use multicolored baby beets if you can find them), but you could also use carrots or even potatoes instead.

Although the ingredient list and method may appear long, this is one of those recipes that can be broken down into distinct parts (when Devin wants a quick dinner, she skips the vegetables and just serves the salmon and drizzle with a green salad). The glaze can be made up to two days ahead (bring it to room temperature before using). The salmon can also be seared ahead (a restaurant chef's trick) and roasted just before serving. The beets, beans and edamame can also be cooked a day ahead.

For the drizzle, in a small bowl, combine the mustard, lemon juice and salt. Let sit for 5 minutes to let the salt dissolve. Slowly whisk in the oil to create an emulsion. Add the garlic and pepper. Set aside, removing the garlic after 30 minutes.

Preheat the oven to 425°F.

For the salmon, rub the fillets with oil and sprinkle with salt and pepper.

Heat a cast-iron skillet or grill pan over high heat and sear the salmon in batches for 1 minute on each side. Place in a roasting pan and set aside.

Bring a saucepan of salted water to a boil. Add the green beans and cook for 4 to 6 minutes, depending on their size (the beans should still be crisp). Submerge in cold water and drain well.

Roast the salmon for 3 to 6 minutes, depending on how well done you like it (3 to 4 minutes for rare, 5 minutes for medium-rare and 6 minutes if you like your salmon cooked all the way through).

While the salmon is roasting, put the oil and shallots in a large cold skillet. Sauté over medium-high heat until the shallots have softened slightly, about 3 minutes. Add the asparagus and continue to cook for 1 minute. Throw in the edamame, green beans and jalapeño and sauté for another minute. Remove from the heat and stir in the herbs, lemon zest and lemon juice. Sprinkle with salt and pepper. Set aside.

Melt the butter in a skillet and sauté the beets for a few minutes, or just until warmed through (you could also heat them up in the microwave).

To serve, divide the green vegetables among six heated shallow bowls. Spoon on the beets and top with a piece of salmon. Pour the drizzle over the salmon and serve.

VEGETABLES

8 oz (250 g) green beans, trimmed (about 1½ cups)

3 Tbsp extra-virgin olive oil

3 Tbsp finely chopped shallots

1 lb (500 g) asparagus, trimmed and cut in thirds

1 cup cooked and shelled edamame, lima or fava beans

½ to 1 tsp finely chopped jalapeño pepper

⅓ cup lightly packed chopped mix of fresh basil, mint and flat-leaf parsley

2 tsp lightly packed grated lemon zest, preferably organic

1 tsp freshly squeezed lemon juice

Sea salt and freshly ground black pepper to taste

1 Tbsp unsalted butter

3 cooked beets (about 1 lb/500 g), peeled and cut in 1-inch chunks

Devin

HONEY-ROASTED HALIBUT ON SOBA NOODLES *with* BOK CHOY *and* MUSHROOMS

SERVES 2

This dish is an impressive dinner-party item and a universal crowd pleaser. My favorite part is the sweet and salty glaze on the halibut, which makes it deceptively rich tasting, although it is actually very light. It's easy to make the soup and noodle base ahead and then bake the fish off at the last minute.

This recipe is written for two (because that's usually how I make it), but just double or triple the ingredients to serve four or six.

HALIBUT

2 Tbsp soy sauce

2 Tbsp liquid honey

1 Tbsp vegetable oil

1 clove garlic, peeled and sliced

2 7-oz (200 g) halibut fillets,
   skin removed

For the halibut, mix together the soy sauce, honey, oil and garlic in a heavy-duty plastic bag. Add the halibut fillets and coat in the marinade. Refrigerate for 1 to 2 hours. Bring the fish to room temperature.

Preheat the oven to 425°F.

NOODLES WITH BOK CHOY AND MUSHROOMS

2 oz (60 g) soba noodles

2 cups chicken stock
   or vegetable stock

¾ tsp grated gingerroot

1 clove garlic, grated

1 Tbsp soy sauce

4 shiitake mushrooms, stemmed and
   cut in quarters

2 baby bok choy, leaves separated

For the noodles, bring a pot of water to a boil. Add the noodles and cook according to the package instructions. Rinse with cold water, drain and set aside.

Bring the chicken stock, ginger, garlic and soy sauce to a boil in a large saucepan.

Remove the fillets from the marinade and place on a baking sheet. Bake the fish for 8 to 12 minutes, or until it is cooked through and a nice caramel color.

While the fish is cooking, add the mushrooms to the stock and simmer for 8 minutes. Add the bok choy and cook for 2 minutes. Add the soba noodles just to warm though.

GARNISH

½ green onion, white and
   light-green part only, finely chopped

½ lime, cut in wedges

Serve the soup in shallow bowls, top with the fish and garnish with green onion and lime.

....

KITCHEN HINT

IS THE FISH DONE?

To test fish for doneness, stick the tip of a sharp knife into the side of a fish fillet for 5 seconds. Immediately touch the tip of the knife to your lip. It should be very warm.

....

Linda

SERVES 4

SALAD

3 cups watermelon, cut in
　½-inch cubes

1½ cups sliced English cucumber
　(seeded and cut in ¼-inch slices)

2 Tbsp finely chopped green onion,
　white and light-green part only

2 Tbsp freshly squeezed lime juice

1 tsp liquid honey

1 tsp hot red pepper flakes

½ tsp kosher salt

¼ tsp freshly ground black pepper

¼ cup lightly packed shredded
　fresh basil

¼ cup lightly packed shredded
　fresh mint

ARCTIC CHAR

4 7-oz (200 g) Arctic char fillets,
　skin on

2 Tbsp extra-virgin olive oil

2 Tbsp freshly squeezed orange juice

¼ tsp kosher salt

¼ tsp freshly ground black pepper

1 lime, cut in quarters, for garnish

GRILLED ARCTIC CHAR *with* LIME-SCENTED WATERMELON *and* CUCUMBER SALAD

When time is of the essence, I make Devin's five-minute cala-mari. When I have time to get to both the fish store and the greengrocer, I like to cook this low-fat fish dish. Make the salad, have a glass of wine, take five minutes to sear the fish and dinner is ready. If you have more time and a bigger appetite, you could start with Devin's sage and pea pasta (page 109) and finish with her chocolate cakes (page 121).

　Red or white snapper or trout can be used if you're not able to find Arctic char.

For the salad, combine the watermelon, cucumber and green onion in a serving bowl.

In a small bowl, combine the lime juice, honey, hot pepper flakes, salt and pepper. Taste and adjust the seasonings, adding a little more honey if needed.

Add the dressing, basil and mint to the salad and toss.

For the Arctic char, score each fillet 3 times just through the skin to keep it from curling when cooking.

In a small bowl, combine the oil and orange juice. Brush both sides of the fish with the mixture and sprinkle with salt and pepper.

Heat a grill pan or cast-iron skillet over high heat. Cook the fish, skin side down, until the sides turn pale pink, about 3 minutes. Carefully flip the fish and cook for another 2 or 3 minutes, or just until cooked through. Place on a dish skin side down and serve with the salad and a wedge of lime.

Devin

FIVE-MINUTE ASIAN GRILLED SQUID

8 cleaned whole squid (about 1¼ to
   1½ lbs/625 to 750 g)

1 clove garlic, grated

½ cup freshly squeezed orange juice

2 Tbsp soy sauce

1 Tbsp liquid honey

½ tsp hot red pepper flakes

½ tsp kosher salt

2 tsp vegetable oil

1 lime, cut in wedges, for garnish

I recommend asking your fishmonger to clean and behead your squid. You will then be left with a white, hollow, rubbery tube that will be easy to cut into half rings before grilling. Once the squid hits the grill, it cooks in a minute, so this is a perfect last-minute recipe.

Don't marinate the squid for more than an hour, as the acid in the orange juice will begin to change the texture of the flesh. This would be perfect served with Mom's fennel and orange salad (page 82).

Using kitchen scissors, snip ½-inch slits crosswise down the body of the squid (1). (Do not cut all the way through the body. It should remain as one whole piece.) When the squid is grilled, it will fan out like a Slinky (2).

In a large bowl, combine the garlic, orange juice, soy sauce, honey, hot pepper flakes and salt. Add the squid and toss in the marinade. Cover with plastic wrap and refrigerate for about 1 hour.

Heat the oil in a grill pan or large skillet over high heat. When the pan is searing hot, add the squid and grill on each side for 30 to 45 seconds, or until opaque.

Serve with lime wedges.

1

2

Linda

SCALLOPS *with* LEEK *and* MOREL RAGOUT

If you're a mushroom fan, you know that springtime heralds morel season. Although they are available dried all year long (and dried work very well in this recipe), there is something deeply satisfying about fresh ones. Leeks, a distant cousin to asparagus, are a natural partner for the earthy mushrooms, and the light covering of cream seems to enhance their flavors.

Both morels and leeks need to be well cleaned of the tiny specks of dirt that hide in their crevices.

Rinse the fresh morels well in cool water. Cut any large mushrooms in half vertically. If you are using dried morels, soak them in hot water for 20 minutes, then drain well.

Place the leeks in a bowl of cold water for 10 minutes to remove any dirt. Drain and pat dry.

Melt the butter in a large skillet over medium heat until it foams. Add the leeks and sauté for about 3 minutes, or until they begin to soften. Add the mushrooms and continue to sauté for 3 minutes.

Pour in the cream, bring to a low boil and simmer gently for about 10 minutes, or until the cream thickens and coats the vegetables. Add the salt and pepper.

Meanwhile, lightly dredge the scallops in flour and sprinkle with salt and pepper.

Heat a large skillet over high heat and add the butter. When the butter stops foaming, add the scallops and cook for 1 to 2 minutes per side, or until they are golden brown and just cooked through. Use more butter if needed.

Spoon the leeks and mushrooms into shallow bowls and top with the scallops and a sprinkling of parsley.

SERVES 4

RAGOUT
20 to 24 large fresh morel
    mushrooms, or ¾ oz (23 g) dried

4 leeks, white and pale-green
    parts only, sliced ¼ inch thick

2 Tbsp unsalted butter

2 cups 35% (whipping) cream

½ tsp kosher salt

⅛ tsp freshly ground white pepper

SCALLOPS
16 large sea scallops

¼ cup unbleached all-purpose flour

½ tsp kosher salt

¼ tsp freshly ground white pepper

2 Tbsp unsalted butter

2 Tbsp lightly packed finely chopped
    fresh flat-leaf parsley

. . . .

KITCHEN HINT

SEA SCALLOPS
Sea scallops are usually about 1½ inches in diameter, while bay scallops grow to about ½ inch. Sea scallops should be pale rosy beige in color and have a sweetish odor. (White scallops sitting in liquid have been processed and frozen.)

For a nice presentation, chefs sometimes cut a crosshatch into scallops before cooking.

. . . .

SERVES 2

AÏOLI

1 large egg yolk, at room temperature

1 Tbsp Dijon mustard

½ tsp kosher salt

¼ tsp freshly ground black pepper

⅛ tsp grated garlic

½ tsp lightly packed finely chopped
   fresh rosemary

½ cup vegetable oil

½ cup extra-virgin olive oil

2 Tbsp freshly squeezed lemon juice
   (about ½ medium)

SHRIMP AND VEGETABLES

10 2-inch fingerling potatoes, skin on
    and cleaned (or cut larger potatoes
    into 2-inch chunks)

6 Tbsp extra-virgin olive oil

1½ tsp kosher salt, divided

½ tsp freshly ground black pepper

3 cloves garlic, peeled and smashed

10 extra-large shrimp, shelled and
    deveined, tails on

1 head radicchio, quartered

8 caper berries, optional

GRILLED SHRIMP *with* CHARRED RADICCHIO, FINGERLINGS *and* AÏOLI

This dish follows the same concept as my mom's scallops (page 137) — a one-dish meal with grilled fish. If you have the opportunity (and budget) to buy fresh morels, then you are a very lucky person! I have a hard time coming across them myself, so I've tried to use ingredients that are easy to find anywhere and at any time of year. Be warned that this is a hearty and fragrant dish with strong flavors, best served with an equally robust red wine or beer.

Grilling lettuce may seem like a strange concept, but it sweetens as it cooks and adds texture and dimension to the dish. You will have some aïoli left over (you'll have more than a cup), but it is also delicious drizzled over any other grilled fish or lightly steamed vegetables. If you don't want to make it from scratch, check out the quick version.

I like to use the big capers on stems in this, but some people hate them; they are totally optional.

For the aïoli, whisk together the egg yolk, mustard, salt, pepper, garlic and rosemary in a bowl. (All the ingredients must be at room temperature in order to emulsify.)

Combine the vegetable oil and olive oil in a small jug or measuring cup.

Now comes the tricky part. You must very, very slowly pour the oil in a thin stream into the egg yolk mixture while whisking vigorously to emulsify the oil with the egg. What you will begin to see (if you are doing it correctly) is a mixture that is very thick, glossy and yellow, with the consistency of custard. Continue to whisk in all the oil.

Finish by whisking in the lemon juice. This will thin out the mixture and change the color to a pale yellow. Set the aïoli aside. (You can also combine the egg yolk, mustard, salt, pepper and garlic in a blender or small food processor. With the food processor running, slowly pour in the oil until the mixture is the consistency of a custard. Transfer to a bowl and whisk in the rosemary and lemon juice.)

For the main dish, place the potatoes in a pot of cold salted water and bring to a boil. Cook for 15 minutes, or until they are tender and cooked through. Drain and set aside.

While the potatoes are cooking, combine the olive oil, 1 tsp salt, pepper and garlic in a measuring cup.

Marinate the shrimp in 3 Tbsp olive oil mixture in a shallow bowl. Brush the radicchio wedges with 2 Tbsp olive oil mixture. Toss the remaining 1 Tbsp olive oil mixture with the cooked potatoes.

Heat a large grill pan over high heat until searing hot. Place the radicchio in the pan and cook for 1 to 2 minutes on each side, or until charred and wilted.

Carefully wipe the pan clean with a paper towel and return to the heat. Cook the shrimp for 1 minute. Flip the shrimp over and add the potatoes to the pan, distributing them among the shrimp. Cook for another 2 minutes, or until the shrimp are no longer transparent in the middle.

Arrange the radicchio in large shallow bowls. Place the shrimp and potatoes on top of the radicchio and top with the caper berries.

Drizzle 2 to 3 Tbsp aïoli over the shrimp and vegetables.

QUICK AND EASY AÏOLI
In a bowl, combine ¾ cup good-quality mayonnaise, 2 Tbsp extra-virgin olive oil, 2 Tbsp freshly squeezed lemon juice, 1 Tbsp Dijon mustard, ⅛ tsp grated garlic, ½ tsp minced fresh rosemary and ¼ tsp freshly ground black pepper.
    Makes about 1¼ cups.

KITCHEN HINT

EMULSIFICATION 101
Emulsification is what happens when you make mayonnaise, and one substance is dispersed into the other in such tiny globules that they stay suspended and don't settle out. Egg can act as an emulsifier. Honey and mustard act as emulsifiers in a vinaigrette.

Linda

SERVES 4 TO 8
(DEPENDING ON APPETITES!)

2 tsp ground cinnamon

1 tsp ground cumin

½ tsp freshly ground black pepper

½ tsp ground allspice

½ tsp chili powder

2 Tbsp vegetable oil

1 Tbsp grated gingerroot

2 tsp grated garlic

4 Cornish hens, butterflied

12 to 14 dried figs

⅓ cup ruby port

3 cooking onions, sliced ½ inch thick

3 oranges, unpeeled and
   sliced ½ inch thick

6 to 8 sprigs of fresh rosemary

1 tsp kosher salt, divided

8 slices bacon, cut in half

½ cup dry white wine

1 Tbsp unsalted butter, cold

MOROCCAN-SPICED CORNISH HENS *with* ROASTED ORANGES, ONIONS *and* FIGS

On a family trip to Morocco, we spent hours wandering the souks. Jewelry and silversmith stores caught our eye, but it was in the spice markets where we spent the most time. Huge mounds of cinnamon, cumin, chilies and mas en harout competed with the mixed spices that are every shopkeeper's specialty.

This was the first meal I cooked when we got home, made with spices we brought back from Morocco.

If you want to use fresh figs, add 6 to 8 during the last 10 minutes of cooking and reduce the port to 3 Tbsp.

Combine the cinnamon, cumin, pepper, allspice, chili powder, oil, ginger and garlic in a small bowl. Rub this paste over both sides of the hens and marinate for 30 minutes at room temperature or for up to 8 hours in the refrigerator. If refrigerated, bring the hens to room temperature before continuing with the recipe.

Toss the dried figs in the port and marinate for at least 1 hour. Drain, reserving the marinade.

Preheat the oven to 425°F.

Combine the onions, oranges, drained figs, rosemary and ¼ tsp salt in a lightly oiled roasting pan.

Arrange the butterflied hens over the fruit and vegetables in one layer. Sprinkle the birds with the remaining ¾ tsp salt and cover each breast and leg with a piece of bacon.

Roast the hens for 15 minutes. Remove the bacon strips and continue to roast the hens for 15 to 20 minutes, or until the juices run clear. Place the birds on a cutting board and tent with foil.

Transfer the fruit and vegetables to a dish and keep warm. Place the roasting pan on the stove over medium-high heat and add the wine and 3 Tbsp reserved port marinade. Cook, stirring, for 1 to 2 minutes, or until syrupy. Remove from the heat and stir in the cold butter and any accumulated juices from the hens. Taste and season with salt and pepper if needed.

Cut each bird in half along the breast bone. Spoon the orange-onion mixture onto a shallow platter, top with the birds (and the bacon, if you wish) and drizzle the glaze over top. Serve 1 or 2 halves per person.

KITCHEN HINT

BUTTERFLYING POULTRY

To butterfly poultry, remove the backbone with kitchen shears or a very sharp knife. Cut down one side of the backbone starting at the cavity between the legs and ending up at the neck. Do the same thing on the other side of the backbone. Discard the backbone, and with the breast side up, press down on the breastbone and flatten the bird against the work surface. (A butcher will also butterfly your birds for you.)

Devin

SESAME CHICKEN *with* MANGO, GREEN ONION *and* GINGER SALSA

Mom's Cornish hens (page 140) are absolutely gorgeous, but they take a little planning, and finding Cornish hens can sometimes be a bit of a mission.

The first time I made this recipe, I defrosted two chicken breasts from my freezer, coated them in sesame seeds, made a quick mango salsa, and dinner was on the table in 25 minutes. What I really love about this meal (other than the fact that it is big-time delicious) is that it looks like something you'd get in a swish restaurant, but your guests will have no idea how easy it was for you to make.

Toss the mango, jalapeño, soy sauce, green onion, coriander, orange zest, orange juice, lime zest, lime juice and salt in a bowl. Taste and add honey if necessary. Let sit at room temperature while you cook the chicken.

Preheat the oven to 400°F.

For the chicken, whisk the egg whites together in a shallow bowl.

In another shallow bowl, stir together the sesame seeds, salt and pepper.

Pat the chicken dry with a paper towel and dip each breast into the egg whites, making sure to coat them thoroughly. Place each chicken breast in the sesame seed mixture and press to coat evenly on all sides. Set the chicken aside.

Heat the butter and oil in a large ovenproof skillet over medium heat. Add the chicken and sear for about 4 minutes, making sure the sesame seeds don't burn. Flip the chicken and place the pan in the oven for 10 to 12 minutes, or until the chicken is cooked through. Cut the chicken into ½-inch slices and serve with a large spoonful of salsa.

SERVES 4

MANGO, GREEN ONION AND GINGER SALSA

1 large ripe mango, peeled and cut in ½-inch cubes

1 tsp finely chopped jalapeño, seeds removed

1 Tbsp soy sauce

1 green onion, white and light-green part only, finely chopped

2 Tbsp lightly packed chopped fresh coriander

1 Tbsp lightly packed grated orange zest, preferably organic

¼ cup freshly squeezed orange juice

½ tsp lightly packed grated lime zest, preferably organic

1 Tbsp freshly squeezed lime juice

1 tsp kosher salt

1 Tbsp liquid honey, optional

SESAME CHICKEN

2 large egg whites

½ cup white sesame seeds

1½ tsp kosher salt

½ tsp freshly ground black pepper

4 boneless, skinless single chicken breasts (about 6 oz/ 175 g each)

1 Tbsp unsalted butter

1 Tbsp vegetable oil

Linda

ROASTED DUCK BREAST
with DRIED CHERRY SHALLOT COMPOTE

3 12-oz (375 g) boneless single
   Magret duck breasts

½ tsp kosher salt

¼ tsp freshly ground black pepper

1 Tbsp vegetable oil

½ cup dry white wine

1 cup finely chopped shallots

1 cup dried cherries

½ cup chicken stock

1 Tbsp unsalted butter

1½ tsp lightly packed chopped
   fresh thyme

4 to 8 sprigs of fresh thyme,
   for garnish

Duck is one of our family favorites, and luckily most butchers now stock it on a regular basis. I find that Magret duck breasts from female birds work best for this dish. The breasts are a good size and the meat is very tender. If the breasts you buy are smaller, use four breasts and reduce the cooking time by a few minutes. The meat should be served medium-rare. Steamed green beans tossed with finely chopped shallots and a knob of butter are a perfect accompaniment. Save the rendered duck fat (you'll decant about a cup) and use it to sauté partially cooked potatoes for a delicious treat.

Preheat the oven to 400°F.

Make two diagonal cuts through the skin on each breast, being careful not to cut into the meat. Sprinkle both sides with salt and pepper.

Heat the oil in a large skillet over medium heat. Place the breasts in the pan skin side down. Reduce the heat slightly and cook for 12 minutes, or until the skin is a dark golden color and has rendered some fat. Remove the breasts from the pan and drain off all but 1 Tbsp fat from the pan.

Return the duck to the skillet and cook, skin side up, for 2 minutes. Remove the meat to baking sheet, skin side up, and roast for 6 minutes.

While the duck is cooking, add the wine to the skillet and cook over high heat, stirring, for about 2 minutes, or until reduced by a quarter. Reduce the heat to medium-high. Add the shallots and dried cherries and cook, stirring, until the pan is almost dry. Don't let the shallots burn.

Add the chicken stock and continue to cook until the stock is almost gone and the shallots are soft, about 4 to 6 minutes.

Stir in the butter and chopped thyme and cook for 1 minute.

Remove the duck from the oven and allow it to rest for
10 minutes. Cut into ¼-inch slices. Fan the slices on a plate
and top with the compote. Garnish with thyme sprigs.

SERVES 4

16 dried apricots

2 Tbsp lightly packed chopped
   fresh sage

3 Tbsp extra-virgin olive oil, divided

4-lb (2 kg) chicken, cut in half,
   with bone and skin still intact

1½ tsp kosher salt

½ tsp freshly ground black pepper

8 paper-thin slices prosciutto

8 fresh sage leaves, ripped in half,
   plus extra leaves for garnish

Devin

ROAST CHICKEN *with*
PROSCIUTTO-WRAPPED APRICOT KEBABS
(photo page 168)

When I asked my mom for her advice on what to make for a small dinner party that I was planning, she suggested her duck with dried cherries (page 144). Not to offend poor Mummy, because I really do love that dish, but I just don't have the time or the money to even think about tackling it.

The thing that I did love about her recipe, though, was the idea of serving some sort of fruit with meat. Using chicken and apricots seemed to be a close substitute that I could still make within my time and budget restraints.

This is a no-fuss twist on traditional roast chicken, and it's soooo easy. I like the fact that you get a little rest time while the chicken is in the oven. Personally, I use this time to have a glass of wine or clean my apartment.

I first tested this recipe on my dad, and he said it was a "humdinger." Take that as you will, but I took it as a compliment.

Ask your butcher to butterfly the chicken for you and then cut it in half along the breast bone, or use Mom's method (page 141). If you are using wooden skewers, soak them in water before using.

Cover the dried apricots with boiling water and set aside for 10 to 15 minutes. (This is an important step to plump up the apricots and make them soft and juicy.)

Preheat the oven to 400°F.

While the apricots are soaking, mix the chopped sage in a small bowl with 2 Tbsp oil.

Gently separate the skin from the breast meat of the chicken, creating small pockets, and rub the sage/oil mixture between the skin and flesh of the chicken. (Don't worry about doing this neatly. It's just to infuse a little extra flavor into the meat.) Rub the top of the skin with the remaining 1 Tbsp oil and sprinkle with salt and pepper.

Place the chicken halves, skin side up, on a baking sheet and pop in the oven for about 40 minutes. You might want to take a peek at the half-hour mark. Depending on the weight of your chicken and your oven, the cooking time can vary slightly. I insert a knife between the breast and the thigh. Mom's rule is that if the juices are still pink, then the chicken needs more time. If they are clear, your chicken is ready.

While the chicken is in the oven, start making your apricot skewers. Remove the apricots from the water and pat them dry. Rip the prosciutto slices in half lengthwise. Wrap a piece around each apricot and divide them among four skewers, placing half a sage leaf between each apricot.

Once the chicken has been in the oven for 20 minutes, brush the skin with some of the pan juices. Add the apricot skewers to the baking pan and let them cook in the chicken juices for the remainder of the cooking time.

When the chicken is done, remove it from the oven and let sit for 10 to 15 minutes to seal all the juices in the meat. Place on a big platter with the apricot skewers and garnish with some extra sage leaves.

SAGE TEA

When I'm feeling a bit anxious after a stressful day, I'll steep some fresh sage leaves in boiling water and drink it as a tea. It helps calm me down instantly (sage tea is also said to counteract swelling, as well as help liver disorders and depression!).

KITCHEN HINT

PRIME PROSCIUTTO

It is well worth buying fresh prosciutto from your deli or butcher counter. You generally want your cured meats to be cut as close to serving time as possible. Cured meats that look brown or dehydrated should be avoided, as they have been cut a long time ago. Prepackaged sliced prosciutto can save you time and money, but keep in mind that it sometimes maintains its color and moisture due to nitrates injected into the packaging.

Linda

VEAL CHOPS ON ROASTED APPLES *and* VEGETABLES *with* HERBED BACON VINAIGRETTE

SERVES 4

VEAL CHOPS

1 clove garlic, grated

1 Tbsp lightly packed finely chopped fresh oregano

1 heaping tsp lightly packed finely chopped fresh rosemary

½ tsp lightly packed finely chopped fresh thyme

2 Tbsp extra-virgin olive oil

⅛ tsp freshly ground black pepper

4 veal chops, about 1¼ inches thick, bone in (about 10 oz/300 g each)

½ tsp kosher salt

My kids ask me to make this when the autumn apples come to the market. The roasted sweetness of carrots and apples is a great counterpoint to the bite of the Brussels sprouts. If you ask your butcher to French the veal bones, you will have a dish worthy of a photo shoot. Pork chops and veal tenderloin can also be used in this recipe.

For the chops, combine the garlic, oregano, rosemary, thyme, oil and pepper in a small bowl. Rub onto both sides of the veal chops and marinate at room temperature for 30 minutes.

Preheat the oven to 400°F.

For the vegetables, combine the onions, carrots, Brussels sprouts, oil, thyme, salt and pepper in a roasting pan in one layer. Roast for about 10 minutes, stirring once, until partially cooked through.

Meanwhile, heat a cast-iron skillet or grill pan over high heat (oil the pan if the chops look a little dry). Sprinkle the chops with salt and sear or grill for 2 minutes per side.

Add the apples to the vegetables and place the chops on top. Continue to roast the vegetables and veal for 10 to 12 minutes, or until the veal is pink and the vegetables are cooked through. Remove the meat to a cutting board and tent with foil. Return the vegetables to the turned-off oven to keep warm.

While the veal is roasting, sauté the bacon in a separate skillet until crisp. Remove the bacon from the pan, leaving the fat. Pour in the wine and vinegar and deglaze the pan over high heat (you should have 2 to 3 Tbsp liquid). Add any liquid from the roasting pan and any juices from the meat and stir in the

Dijon, powdered mustard and oil. Add the bacon pieces at the last minute, as they should be served as crisp as possible.

Place the vegetables on a serving dish and top with the veal chops and bacon vinaigrette.

BARBECUED VEAL CHOPS WITH
GRILLED PEACHES AND BALSAMIC

Combine 2 Tbsp extra-virgin olive oil, 1 Tbsp balsamic vinegar and ½ tsp freshly ground black pepper in a bowl. Add 4 pitted and halved peaches, and toss.

Grill 4 veal chops. Remove to a platter and tent with foil. Place the peach halves skin side up on the barbecue and grill for about 2 minutes, or until they have softened slightly and grill marks appear.

Serve the chops with the grilled peaches and sprinkle with shredded fresh basil and mint.

Serves 4.

. . . .

KITCHEN HINT

FRENCHED CHOPS

When you ask butchers to French a chop, they will scrape the meat off the bone to expose it. Some cooks like to wrap the exposed bone in foil during cooking so the bone is a pale beige when the foil is removed.

. . . .

VEGETABLES AND APPLES

3 cooking onions, peeled and quartered

6 to 8 carrots, peeled and cut in 1-inch chunks on the diagonal

16 large Brussels sprouts, trimmed and cut in half

3 Tbsp extra-virgin olive oil

½ tsp lightly packed finely chopped fresh thyme

½ tsp kosher salt

¼ tsp freshly ground black pepper

2 Spy or Granny Smith apples, unpeeled, cored and cut in ½-inch wedges

VINAIGRETTE

4 slices bacon, cut in ½-inch pieces

¼ cup dry red wine

3 Tbsp red wine vinegar

2 tsp Dijon mustard

¼ tsp powdered mustard

3 Tbsp extra-virgin olive oil

SERVES 4

GLAZED DATES

½ cup cider vinegar

½ cup beer

2 Tbsp lightly packed chopped
  fresh thyme

16 dates, pitted and quartered

½ tsp Worcestershire sauce

4 cloves garlic, grated

2 Tbsp unsalted butter, cold

PORK CHOPS

¼ cup all-purpose flour

2 tsp kosher salt

½ tsp freshly ground black pepper

8 small bone-in pork rib chops
  (about 5 oz/150 g each), about
  ½ inch thick

2 Tbsp unsalted butter, divided

2 Tbsp extra-virgin olive oil, divided

SWEET *and* STICKY PORK CHOPS *with* GLAZED DATES

This is everything the name implies. Succulent and juicy, it's one sexy dish — especially delectable on a chilly winter night. The cider vinegar and beer add a bit of bite to the rich pork, and the sweet dates give this a luscious touch. Serve the chops on a bed of pink couscous.

For the glazed dates, combine the vinegar, beer, thyme, dates, Worcestershire sauce and garlic in a bowl.

For the pork chops, in a shallow bowl, mix together the flour, salt and pepper.

Dredge each pork chop in the flour, shaking off any excess. Set aside.

Heat 1 Tbsp butter and 1 Tbsp oil in a large skillet over medium-high heat until the mixture just begins to brown.

Add 4 pork chops to the skillet and sear for 4 minutes on each side, or until browned and cooked through. Place on a serving platter and keep warm. Cook the last 4 chops in the remaining 1 Tbsp butter and 1 Tbsp oil and remove to the platter.

Return the skillet to medium-low heat and add the date mixture. Simmer for 3 minutes. Add the 2 Tbsp cold butter and stir just to melt (adding cold butter makes the sauce nice and shiny). Spoon the dates over the pork chops.

PEARLY PINK ISRAELI COUSCOUS

Boiling the couscous in beet juice gives this dish its bright magenta color, which looks amazing on a white plate. It's also fun for a special occasion like Valentine's Day. Beet juice is available at most health food stores, but if you can't find it, you can use the liquid from canned beets.

Combine 1 cup beet juice, ⅓ cup water, ½ tsp kosher salt and 1 peeled and crushed garlic clove in a saucepan. Bring to a boil. Stir in 1 cup Israeli couscous and reduce the heat to low. Cover and cook for 10 to 12 minutes, or until the couscous has absorbed all the liquid and is *al dente*. Stir once or twice while it is cooking. Remove the garlic and stir in 1 Tbsp extra-virgin olive oil. Serve immediately.

Serves 4.

Linda

SERVES 6

LAMB

2½-lb (1 kg) butterflied leg of lamb

3 cloves garlic, grated

1½ tsp dried mint

1 Tbsp lightly packed finely chopped
    fresh oregano

2 Tbsp extra-virgin olive oil

¼ tsp freshly ground black pepper

CHUTNEY

½ large sweet white onion, peeled and
    cut in 5 wedges through the core

5 nectarines, unpeeled, pitted and
    cut in quarters

1½ Tbsp extra-virgin olive oil

1 tsp sherry vinegar

⅓ cup red wine vinegar

¼ cup granulated sugar

1 Tbsp lightly packed chopped
    fresh oregano

½ tsp freshly ground black pepper

1 sprig of fresh mint

1 Tbsp lightly packed finely
    chopped fresh mint

BUTTERFLIED LEG OF LAMB *with* GRILLED NECTARINE *and* ONION CHUTNEY

I always hope for leftover lamb when I make this recipe. For lunch the next day, I spread a generous layer of hummos on a warm roll and top it with grilled eggplant and zucchini, lamb, some mint leaves and crunchy lettuce. Devin prefers to forgo the hummos and instead chops the mint into mayonnaise to use as a spread.

Grilling the nectarines and onion adds a smoky goodness to this chutney. You will have more than you need. Extra chutney is delicious served with grilled pork tenderloin and roast chicken. It will keep in the refrigerator for a couple of days.

To prepare the lamb, place it fat side up in a roasting pan. Combine the garlic, dried mint, oregano, oil and pepper in a small bowl. Massage into both sides of the lamb. Cover and refrigerate for 45 minutes at room temperature or up to 10 hours in the refrigerator. Bring to room temperature before roasting.

Preheat the oven to 425°F.

To prepare the chutney, toss the onion and the nectarines in the olive oil. Place on a hot barbecue or grill pan in batches and cook until nicely charred but not cooked through.

Toss the onions in a bowl with the sherry vinegar. Roughly chop the onions and nectarines and place them in a shallow baking dish. Stir in the red wine vinegar, sugar, oregano, pepper and mint sprig.

Bake the chutney for 30 minutes. Cool to room temperature, remove the mint sprig and stir in the finely chopped mint.

Roast the lamb for 16 to 18 minutes for medium-rare (14 to 16 minutes for rare). Let sit, lightly covered, for 10 to 20 minutes before slicing. (You can also grill the lamb for 7 to 8 minutes per side.) Serve the lamb with the chutney.

SERVES 4

CHIMICHURRI

⅓ cup extra-virgin olive oil

⅓ cup warm water

⅓ cup white wine vinegar

2 tsp grated garlic

1 green onion, white and light-green part only, finely chopped

½ large green bell pepper, seeded and finely chopped (about ⅔ cup)

1 small tomato, seeded and finely chopped (about ½ cup)

2 Tbsp lightly packed finely chopped fresh flat-leaf parsley

2 tsp lightly packed finely chopped fresh oregano

2 tsp kosher salt

1 tsp sweet paprika

¾ tsp ground cumin

½ tsp chili powder

½ tsp freshly ground black pepper

FLANK STEAK

6 cloves garlic, peeled and smashed

⅔ cup freshly squeezed orange juice (about 2 medium)

½ cup dry red wine

¼ cup extra-virgin olive oil

½ tsp freshly ground black pepper

1½ lbs (750 g) flank steak

1 Tbsp vegetable oil

ARGENTINIAN FLANK STEAK *with* CARAMELIZED ONIONS *and* CHIMICHURRI

Steak is a way of life in Argentina; it's part of everyone's diet. The typical sauce that is served with it is called chimichurri, and it is as common on tables as salt and pepper. It's an amazing tangy green salsa with lots of herbs and vinegar, which makes it a fantastic partner for steak. After we came back from a vacation in Buenos Aires, my mom and I went on a mission to recreate it.

I love making flank steak for company. It's inexpensive, and it's an easy way to feed a crowd (always serve it rare or medium-rare). Make the chimichurri a day ahead; you'll probably have more than you need, but it should keep in the refrigerator for up to a month.

For the chimichurri, combine the olive oil, water, vinegar, garlic, green onion, green pepper, tomato, parsley, oregano, salt, paprika, ground cumin, chili powder and pepper in a bowl or jar. The liquid should just cover the vegetables and herbs. Add equal amounts of oil, water and vinegar if needed. Cover and refrigerate for 12 to 24 hours. (It can also be served immediately, but the flavor will not be as interesting.)

For the steak, combine the garlic, orange juice, wine, olive oil and pepper in a large shallow dish. Add the steak and flip a few times in the marinade to coat. Cover with plastic wrap and marinate in the refrigerator for 1 to 2 hours. Remove the meat from the fridge 30 to 45 minutes before grilling.

While the meat is coming to room temperature, make the caramelized onions. Heat the olive oil in a large skillet over high heat. Add the onions, cumin seeds, salt and pepper and sauté for a couple of minutes. Reduce the heat to medium-high and add the orange juice. Cook, stirring frequently, for about 30 minutes, or until the onions are golden. Add the red wine and cook for 3 minutes longer. Remove from the heat and set aside.

Preheat the oven to 400°F. Remove the steak from the marinade and pat dry.

Heat the vegetable oil in a grill pan over high heat. If you are using a barbecue, heat to high heat and lightly brush the meat with the oil.

Sear the steak for 3 minutes on each side (to create a crosshatch pattern on the steak, rotate it halfway through cooking on each side). Remove the steak from the grill and place it on a baking sheet. Roast in the oven for 3 to 5 minutes for medium-rare, or until a meat thermometer inserted into the thickest part of the meat registers 120 to 124°F (49 to 51°C). Allow the meat to rest on a cutting board loosely covered with foil for 10 to 15 minutes (the meat will continue to cook as it sits) before cutting it into long thin slices against the grain.

Return the onions to high heat for 2 minutes to warm. Spread the onions on a large platter and top with the sliced steak. Serve the chimichurri on the side.

. . . .

KITCHEN HINT

GRILLING STEAK

Make sure that your meat is at room temperature before grilling. Never cook steak that is even partially frozen or straight from the fridge. You will end up with a burnt exterior and raw interior. Turn your meat with tongs, as a fork will puncture the meat, and juices will be lost.

. . . .

CARAMELIZED ONIONS

¼ cup extra-virgin olive oil

4 large cooking onions, thinly sliced

½ tsp cumin seeds

1 tsp kosher salt

¼ tsp freshly ground black pepper

⅓ cup freshly squeezed orange juice (about 1 medium)

½ cup dry red wine

Linda

AIX-EN-PROVENCE BLACK OLIVE TART

This easy-to-make tart is reason enough to invest in a 12-inch fluted tart pan with a removable bottom. This is my simplified take on a tart that was served to us on a hot summer day in the south of France. The olive oil in the crust makes for a flaky casing and because it can be pressed into the tin, even a pastry klutz like me can produce spectacular results. You can replace the endive with spinach, radicchio or Chinese cabbage, or try a combination. I serve it warm or at room temperature with a warm baguette, roasted tomatoes and a simple arugula salad or Devin's watercress salad (page 79).

For the pastry, put the flour, salt, butter, egg yolk and 3 Tbsp oil in the bowl of a food processor. Pulse until it just comes together. Add the extra tablespoon of oil if necessary. (If you are mixing by hand, put the flour, salt and butter in a bowl and toss together. Add the egg and 3 Tbsp oil and mix together with your hands. Add the extra tablespoon of oil if needed to bring the dough together. The dough should be crumbly.)

Form the dough into a flattened disc, wrap in plastic wrap and refrigerate for 30 minutes.

Roll the dough between 2 pieces of parchment paper or plastic wrap into a rough 15-inch circle. This may prove difficult as the dough is very crumbly, but don't worry. Just pat the dough evenly into the bottom and sides of a 12-inch fluted tart pan with a removable bottom. Chill for at least 30 minutes. (The dough can be made and patted into the pan up to a day ahead.)

Preheat the oven to 400°F.

To prepare the filling, whisk the eggs and crème fraîche in a bowl.

Add the oil and onions to a large cold skillet and heat over medium-high heat. Sauté until the onions are soft but not colored, about 10 to 12 minutes.

SERVES 8

OLIVE-OIL PASTRY

2 cups plus 3 Tbsp unbleached all-purpose flour

Pinch of kosher salt

¾ cup unsalted butter, cold, cut in ¼-inch cubes

1 large egg yolk, beaten

3 to 4 Tbsp extra-virgin olive oil

FILLING

2 large eggs

3 Tbsp crème fraîche (page 201) or 35% (whipping) cream

¼ cup extra-virgin olive oil

2 small cooking onions, cut in half and thinly sliced

1 lb (500 g) Belgian endive, cut in ½-inch slices

3 cloves garlic, finely chopped (about 2½ tsp)

½ tsp finely chopped fresh thyme

¾ cup pitted Kalamata olives, cut in half if large

¼ tsp kosher salt

Heaping ⅛ tsp freshly ground black pepper

6 to 8 oven-roasted tomatoes, cut in half (page 158)

Add the endive, garlic and thyme. Cook until the endive is slightly wilted and the pan is almost dry, about 3 to 4 minutes. Remove from the heat and stir in the olives, egg mixture, salt and pepper. Immediately pour into the tart shell, making sure the olives are evenly distributed. (For a nice finish, brush the exposed crust with a little extra olive oil.)

Bake for 50 minutes, or until the filling is just set in the center. Remove from the oven and let cool for 15 minutes. Top with oven-roasted tomatoes.

OVEN-ROASTED TOMATOES

Cut 8 plum tomatoes in half lengthwise and toss with ⅓ cup balsamic vinegar, 2 Tbsp soy sauce and 1 Tbsp vegetable oil. Marinate for a couple of hours at room temperature or overnight in the refrigerator.

   Place the tomatoes, cut side up, on a foil-covered baking sheet. Bake in a preheated 300°F oven for 1 to 1½ hours, or until the tomatoes are shriveled around the edges but not dried out. Extra tomatoes will keep, covered, in the refrigerator for up to a week. (They're fabulous in a classic ACE Bakery sandwich layered with caramelized onions and Asiago cheese on rosemary focaccia.)

Devin

THREE-CHEESE PUFF PASTRY TART

SERVES 8 AS A MAIN COURSE;
16 AS AN APPETIZER

You really won't believe how incredibly good this is. It is a great buffet addition for any veggie friends. My sister, Lindsey, who hasn't touched so much as a measly chicken wing since she was sixteen, is very appreciative when I make this tart for family lunches. It's fantastic served with Mom's sweet greens and persimmon salad (page 78).

Gently place the squares of pastry on a parchment-lined baking sheet (you might need two baking sheets). Trim 1 inch off each side of the squares and set aside. Brush the beaten egg along the outside edges of the squares and place the strips back on top to create a double-layered pastry wall around the square. Press down along the edges with your fingers to make sure the dough sticks together. Prick the surface of the dough with a fork and refrigerate for 15 minutes.

Mix together the mascarpone, chives, salt and pepper in a bowl. Spread evenly over the surface of the chilled pastry, staying within the pastry edges.

Place the Brie slices over the mascarpone in a diagonal pattern. You may have to trim a few pieces to fit. Sprinkle with the grated Parmesan. Return the tarts to the fridge for 10 minutes.

Preheat the oven to 375°F.

Brush the edges of the pastry with the oil and bake for 30 to 35 minutes, or until the pastry is cooked and the cheese is golden (I like to remove the tarts from the baking sheet halfway through the baking time and place them directly on the oven rack to help the pastry bottom cook all the way through.) If the pastry base bubbles up while baking, prick it with a knife to deflate.

2 8-oz (250 g) sheets prerolled puff pastry, about 10 inches square

1 large egg, lightly beaten

1 cup mascarpone cheese

2 Tbsp lightly packed chopped fresh chives

½ tsp kosher salt

¼ tsp freshly ground pepper

7 oz (200 g) ripe Brie, cut in slices about 2 inches long and ¼ inch thick

1 cup coarsely grated Parmesan cheese (about 3½ oz/100 g)

2 Tbsp extra-virgin olive oil

KITCHEN HINT

PUFF PASTRY — BUTTER IS BEST
I like to buy prerolled puff pastry sheets. You can find them in most grocery stores and they are really easy to use. You can also buy all-butter puff pastry from a patisserie or specialty store. It will usually come in one large 1-lb (500 g) block, so you will need to roll it out yourself (roll it out on a floured surface until it is about ⅛ inch thick, and be sure to rotate the pastry after every three or four turns of the rolling pin to prevent sticking).

Linda

SERVES 6 TO 8

3 Tbsp pine nuts

1 medium lemon, preferably organic

2½-lb (1 kg) head cauliflower,
trimmed and broken in florets
(about 1¾ lbs/875 g trimmed,
or 6 to 7 cups)

¼ cup unsalted butter

½ tsp kosher salt

¼ tsp freshly ground black pepper

CAULIFLOWER *with* BROWN BUTTER, PINE NUTS *and* LEMON

Try this with Devin's roast chicken (page 146) when you've had enough of cauliflower with cheese sauce. The nutty brown butter combined with the delicate but crunchy pine nuts and the sparkle of lemon zest will make you appreciate cauliflower in a whole new way.

Toast the pine nuts in a small dry skillet over medium heat, shaking or stirring frequently, for 4 to 5 minutes, or until golden.

Zest the lemon using very broad strokes. You want long thin zest, so don't use a microplane zester.

Bring a large pot of salted water to a boil. Add the cauliflower and cook for 5 to 7 minutes, or until just tender.

While the cauliflower is cooking, melt the butter in a small saucepan. Simmer over low heat for a few minutes, or until the butter foams and then turns golden brown. Strain through a fine sieve and return the butter to the saucepan.

Drain the cauliflower and transfer to a serving bowl. Reheat the butter if necessary and pour over the cauliflower. Add the salt and pepper and toss gently. Sprinkle with pine nuts and lemon zest and serve immediately.

Devin

CHARRED BROCCOLI
with SPICED YOGURT

I had a version of this recipe at a fantastic Indian restaurant while I was living in London. I loved it so much that I had two more orders . . . seriously! I created my own delicious adaptation the next day and it has now become my go-to side dish. Don't skimp on the whole milk yogurt — it really makes all the difference.

You may not need all of the spiced yogurt. Any leftovers are delicious on any grilled meat or fish.

Preheat the broiler.

For the yogurt, combine the yogurt, honey, salt, cinnamon and hot pepper flakes in a small bowl. Set aside.

Toss the broccoli, oil, salt, cumin and cinnamon on a foil-lined baking sheet (to save on cleanup) until evenly coated. Spread in a single layer.

Place the broccoli about 3 inches from the broiler element and broil for 5 minutes, or until the broccoli is tender and has beautiful char marks. Keep an eye on it; you want to have blackened edges on the broccoli, but be careful not to totally burn it.

Transfer the broccoli to a serving bowl. Spoon the yogurt over top and serve warm.

SERVES 4

SPICED YOGURT
1½ cups whole-milk yogurt,
    at room temperature

1 tsp liquid honey

½ tsp kosher salt

⅛ tsp ground cinnamon

Pinch of hot red pepper flakes

CHARRED BROCCOLI
1 large bunch broccoli (about
    1¼ lbs/625 g),
    broken in large florets

¼ cup vegetable oil

½ tsp kosher salt

¼ tsp ground cumin

⅛ tsp ground cinnamon

Linda

CORN TOSS
(photo page 168)

(photo page 168)

5 ears corn, husked

1½ Tbsp vegetable oil

1 small cooking onion, finely chopped

1 clove garlic, finely chopped

1 small zucchini (about 5 inches long),
    seeded and cut in slices
    ¼ inch thick

1 tomato, seeded and
    roughly chopped

½ tsp kosher salt

¼ tsp freshly ground black pepper

5 to 6 fresh basil leaves, torn

The perfect time to whip up this recipe is in July and August when farmers' markets and roadside stands are brimming with luscious, just-picked corn. To make life easier for yourself, prep the vegetables and sauté the onions and garlic. Let the pan cool a bit and pile in everything except the basil. Minutes before you plan to eat, put the pan over medium-high heat and cook, stirring every once in awhile until the corn and zucchini are cooked but still a bit crispy.

When my children were small I would toss in some finely cubed Monterey Jack or mozzarella before adding the basil – a sure-fire way to get kids to eat their veggies.

Stand the corn, stem side down, in a shallow bowl. Run a sharp knife down the side of the corn between the kernels and the cob to remove the kernels. You should have 4 to 5 cups.

Add the oil and onion to a large cold skillet. Heat over medium heat and sauté the onion until it is soft and pale golden, about 5 to 7 minutes. Add the garlic and cook for 30 seconds.

Stir in the corn, zucchini and tomato. Increase the heat to medium-high and sauté until the corn and zucchini are just cooked through but still crisp. Season with salt and pepper and stir in the basil.

Devin

HUSK-ON ROASTED CORN
with CHIPOTLE LIME BUTTER

This is a great make-ahead recipe. You can assemble the butter the night before and even rub it on the corn to sit overnight in the fridge before baking. Don't be alarmed when the husks brown or even blacken in the oven. It has nothing to do with the doneness of the actual corn.

These are also great grilled on the barbecue.

Preheat the oven to 450°F.

Combine the butter, chipotle, lime zest, lime juice and salt in a small bowl.

Gently pull the husk away from the corn without detaching it from the bottom. Remove the silk and discard. (Use a damp paper towel to rub off any extra silk easily.) Using your hands, rub the flavored butter generously over the corn. Pull the husk back up over the corn and twist it together at the top. To prevent them from smoking, dampen the husks with a wet paper towel before putting them in the oven.

Place the husks on a baking sheet and bake for 15 minutes. The husks will brown and might even blacken slightly.

Serve the corn with the husk on and let guests remove it before eating.

HUSK-ON ROASTED CORN WITH
TWO CHEESES, GARLIC AND CHIVES
Combine ½ cup mascarpone cheese, ⅓ cup lightly packed grated Parmesan cheese, ½ grated clove garlic, 2 Tbsp lightly packed finely chopped fresh chives, ½ tsp kosher salt and ¼ tsp freshly ground black pepper in a small bowl. Spread on the corn instead of the chipotle lime butter.

SERVES 4

½ cup unsalted butter,
   at room temperature

1½ Tbsp finely chopped chipotle
   pepper (about 1 canned chipotle)

½ tsp lightly packed grated lime zest,
   preferably organic

1 Tbsp freshly squeezed lime juice

½ tsp kosher salt

4 ears corn, unhusked

Linda

SLOW-COOKED RED CABBAGE
with SWEET APPLE

SERVES 12

⅓ cup vegetable oil

1 red cabbage (about 2½ lbs/1 kg),
    trimmed and thinly shredded

½ cup red wine vinegar

1 cup dry red wine

1 cup beef stock

5 bay leaves

1 cooking onion, peeled

20 cloves

1 tsp granulated sugar

¾ tsp kosher salt

¼ tsp freshly ground black pepper

3 large apples (e.g., Northern Spy,
    Golden Delicious or Spy)

Think of this as a beautiful cold-weather staple to serve with turkey, ham or pot roast. My friend Mechtild, who introduced me to braised cabbage, uses lard instead of vegetable oil to start the dish. For a rich, hearty flavor you could cook with bacon fat, keeping the bacon to crumble over the top. This recipe serves twelve, but you can freeze any leftovers.

Heat the oil over medium heat in a large saucepan. Add the cabbage and sauté for 5 to 6 minutes, or until it is warm and coated with oil.

Stir in the vinegar, wine and stock. (There should be about ½ to 1 inch of liquid in the bottom of the saucepan.) Throw in the bay leaves.

Stud the onion with the cloves and add it to the pot. Add the sugar, salt and pepper. Cover and simmer for about 45 minutes, or until the cabbage is fairly soft.

Peel and core the apples and cut them into ½-inch cubes. Stir them into the cabbage and cook until the apples are soft but still retain their shape, about 10 to 15 minutes. Taste and add sugar, salt or pepper if needed. Remove the clove-studded onion and bay leaves before serving.

Devin

SHREDDED BRUSSELS SPROUTS *with* CRANBERRIES, PECANS *and* SHALLOTS

SERVES 4 TO 6

Even people who don't like Brussels sprouts will love these! They are super quick to make, and the sweet dried cranberries and pecans mellow out the sometimes bitter Brussels sprout flavor. Shredding the sprouts makes them look and taste kind of like shredded cabbage, and baking them in a hot oven is quicker than Mom's slow-cooked cabbage.

1 lb (500 g) Brussels sprouts, trimmed

⅔ cup chopped pecans

½ cup dried cranberries

1 shallot, finely chopped

1 tsp kosher salt

¼ tsp freshly ground black pepper

1 Tbsp extra-virgin olive oil

Preheat the oven to 425°F.

Slice the Brussels sprouts lengthwise as thinly as possible (about ⅛ inch) using a very sharp knife. Some of the rounds will stay together and some will fall apart, which is fine.

Toss the sprouts, pecans, cranberries, shallot, salt, pepper and oil on a large baking sheet.

Bake for 15 minutes, or until some of the edges begin to brown. Serve warm.

Linda

SERVES 6

1 medium red onion, cut in
   half and thinly sliced

2 zucchini (about 7 to 8 inches long),
   thinly sliced in rounds on the
   diagonal

10 small tomatoes, thinly sliced

½ tsp lightly packed finely chopped
   fresh thyme

Heaping ¼ tsp kosher salt

Heaping ⅛ tsp freshly ground
   black pepper

2 Tbsp extra-virgin olive oil

3 Tbsp lightly packed grated
   Parmesan cheese, optional

PROVENÇAL TOMATO, ONION *and* ZUCCHINI GRATIN

Every Provençal cook has a version of this rustic and attractive summer classic. Most French cooks slice the vegetables paper thin, which calls for an extremely sharp knife and a lot of patience, but ¼-inch slices are just fine. Be sure to line the rows of vegetables down the longest side of your dish and stay within the amount of tomato, onion and zucchini called for in the recipe. (Whenever I've overloaded the vegetables I end up with a pool of liquid in the bottom of the pan.)

If you can't imagine a gratin without cheese, sprinkle the top with grated Parmesan before the last 15 minutes of baking. Serve it at room temperature with cold chicken or grilled fish in the heat of summer and warm with roasted lamb or sausages when the weather turns cooler. It's also terrific on its own with a piece of good Camembert and a good-quality baguette.

Preheat the oven to 400°F.

Alternate onion, zucchini and tomato slices in rows in a lightly oiled 13- by 9-inch baking dish. The vegetables should overlap a fair bit so that they almost stand up in the dish. You should have three or four rows.

Sprinkle with thyme, salt and pepper and drizzle with oil. Bake for 30 minutes. (If you are using cheese, sprinkle it on after 15 minutes.) Serve hot or at room temperature.

Devin

ZUCCHINI RIBBONS *with* TOASTED GARLIC ANCHOVY BREADCRUMBS

SERVES 4

I know you've heard this one before, but the anchovy taste really does completely disappear when it is cooked, leaving behind an amazing rich salty flavor that gives this dish real oomph. For plating, pile your zucchini ribbons in a mounded rippling tower, topped with the breadcrumbs (as in the photo).

If you can't find yellow zucchini, just use all green.

Mix together the garlic, anchovies and breadcrumbs in a small bowl. Set aside.

Using a vegetable peeler, shave long "ribbons" off the sides of the zucchini (it helps if you rotate the zucchini a quarter turn once you reach the seeds). You want to make sure that you get as much of the colored skin on each ribbon as possible. Discard the core and set the ribbons aside.

Heat 2 Tbsp oil in a large skillet over high heat. Add the breadcrumb mixture and stir continuously until golden and fragrant, about 2 minutes.

Remove the breadcrumbs from the pan and set aside. Carefully wipe any extra crumbs from the hot pan with a paper towel.

Return the pan to the high heat and add the remaining oil. Sauté the zucchini with the salt and pepper for 2 minutes, until just cooked but still slightly crisp.

Serve the zucchini topped with the anchovy breadcrumbs.

2 cloves garlic, grated

6 anchovy fillets, minced

1 cup fresh breadcrumbs (page 105)

2 medium yellow zucchini (about 1 lb/500 g total)

2 medium green zucchini (about 1 lb/500 g total)

¼ cup extra-virgin olive oil, divided

½ tsp kosher salt

¼ tsp freshly ground black pepper

SERVES 6

1½ lbs (750 g) Jerusalem artichokes

¼ cup freshly squeezed lemon juice
(about 1 medium), divided

1 small celery root (about 8 oz/250 g)

¾ tsp kosher salt

½ small sweet onion (about
3½ oz/100 g), thinly sliced

⅛ tsp freshly ground white pepper

2¼ cups 35% (whipping) cream

3 cups fresh breadcrumbs (page 105)

1 cup lightly packed finely grated
Parmesan cheese (about 3 oz/90 g)

Linda

JERUSALEM ARTICHOKE, ONION *and* CELERY ROOT GRATIN *with* PARMESAN CRUST

Jerusalem artichokes, also called sunchokes, are the tubers of a species of sunflower. High in fiber and a good source of potassium, vitamin C and folate, they have a delicate taste (like a water chestnut with a hint of artichoke) that plays well with the celery root.

Preheat the oven to 400°F.

Peel the Jerusalem artichokes if the skin is thick. If they are young and thin-skinned, just scrub them well with a vegetable brush. Slice thinly and place in a large bowl. Cover them with cold water and 2 Tbsp lemon juice to prevent discoloring.

Peel the celery root and cut it in half. Slice it thinly and add to the Jerusalem artichokes.

Drain the vegetables and pat dry when you are ready to assemble the gratin. Working quickly, cover the bottom of a very lightly buttered 10-cup baking dish with an overlapping layer of half the Jerusalem artichokes. Sprinkle with ¼ tsp salt. Cover with all the onion and then an overlapping layer of celery root. Sprinkle with another ¼ tsp salt. Finish with the remaining Jerusalem artichokes. Sprinkle with the rest of the salt and all the pepper.

Warm the cream in a small saucepan or in the microwave. Whisk in the remaining lemon juice and pour the cream over the vegetables.

Bake for 35 to 40 minutes, or until the vegetables are just tender.

Meanwhile, in a bowl, combine the breadcrumbs and cheese. Top the vegetables with the breadcrumb mixture and bake for 15 to 20 minutes. Cover loosely with foil if the top becomes too dark. Let the casserole sit for 10 minutes before serving.

Devin

APPLE *and* CHEDDAR
SCALLOPED POTATOES

Scalloped potatoes are one of my all-time favorite foods. Mom has always made them with mounds and mounds of Gruyère cheese, which is delectable but a little pricy. Cheddar, the unsung hero of cheeses, is amazing in this dish when paired with its old friend the apple. You can use any Cheddar you like, from an aged white to a mild yellow, but I personally prefer something on the stronger side.

Preheat the oven to 400°F.

Combine the cream and garlic in a jug or large measuring cup.

Peel the potatoes and cut into rounds ⅛ inch thick. Peel and core the apples and cut into wedges ¼ inch thick.

Place one overlapping layer of potato in the bottom of a generously buttered 8-cup shallow baking dish. Sprinkle one quarter of the salt and pepper over the potatoes and top with one quarter of the cheese and one quarter of the cream mixture.

Arrange all the apple slices over the potatoes in one overlapping layer. Top with one quarter of the salt, pepper and cheese and one quarter of the cream mixture.

Make two more layers of potatoes, alternating with the salt, pepper, cheese and cream.

Loosely cover with foil and place on a baking sheet. Bake for 20 minutes. Remove the foil and bake for 35 to 40 minutes, or until the potatoes are tender and the top is golden. Let sit for 10 minutes before serving.

SERVES 8

2 cups 35% (whipping) cream

2 cloves garlic, grated

4 baking potatoes (about
  10 oz/300 g each)

2 Granny Smith apples

1 tsp kosher salt

½ tsp freshly ground black pepper

2½ cups grated Cheddar cheese
  (about 10 oz/300 g)

Linda

24 carrots (about 2½ lbs/1 kg)

2 Tbsp unsalted butter

4 to 6 Tbsp Marsala

Pinch of kosher salt

Pinch of freshly ground white pepper

1 Tbsp lightly packed finely
  chopped fresh parsley, optional

. . . .

KITCHEN HINT

MARSALA MAGIC

Marsala, a beautiful amber-colored for-
tified wine, originated in Sicily, where
brandy was added to wine to give it
a longer shelf life. Kegs of wine are
stacked on top of each other, and wine
from the bottom kegs is refreshed with
liquid from a keg above until the fer-
mentation process is complete.

There are five categories of Marsala,
ranging from sweet to dry. Traditionally served at room temperature as an
aperitif between the first and second
course, it is equally delicious as an
accompaniment to Parmesan, Gor-
gonzola or Roquefort and as a compan-
ion to most desserts. If you can't find it,
substitute Madeira.

. . . .

SWEET BUTTER CARAMELIZED CARROTS *with* MARSALA GLAZE

These deceptively simple but elegant carrots are cooked and ready
to head to the table in just a few minutes. Please buy bunch carrots
with the stems attached. If you can only find large prepackaged
carrots, cut them in quarters lengthwise. You can peel and slice
the carrots and lay them in the melted butter hours before they
are to be served. Put the lid on the pan and remove from the heat
until you're ready to continue with the recipe.

This may be the time to buy a tiny bottle of Marsala usually
available at the checkout counter at liquor stores. Or you could buy
a big bottle and read the hint on how to drink the rest!

Peel and cut the carrots in half lengthwise, leaving a touch of
green at the top. (If the carrots are less than ½ inch thick at the
top, leave them whole.)

Melt the butter in a large skillet over medium-high heat.

Place the carrots in the pan (no more than a double layer, so
you may need to use two pans) and cover. Cook for 2 minutes,
then shake the pan to make sure the carrots aren't sticking to
the bottom. Reduce the heat to medium and continue to cook
for 8 to 12 minutes, or until the carrots are tender (it's fine if
they have caramelized a little). Shake the pan two or three
times while they are cooking and add a little water if the pan
seems dry.

Pour in the Marsala. Cook, uncovered, until there is a thin
glaze covering the carrots, about 1 minute.

Sprinkle with salt, pepper and parsley before serving.

Devin

SWEET POTATO, SPINACH
and GOAT CHEESE GRATIN

When I made this, my brother, Luke, joked that it was the Irish version of scalloped potatoes because its orange, white and green layers resembled the Irish flag. I pointed out that sweet potatoes, spinach and goat cheese are not native to Ireland, but that we Irish would love it anyway.

All jokes aside, this is a great light alternative to scalloped potatoes. It is low in fat and extremely nutritious.

Preheat the oven to 400°F.

Peel the sweet potatoes and, with a large knife, cut them into rounds ⅛ inch thick.

Combine the garlic and oil in a small bowl.

Brush a layer of garlic oil over the bottom and sides of a 6-cup round baking dish.

Place a layer of overlapping sweet potato slices in the bottom of the dish. Drizzle with 1 Tbsp garlic oil. Top with one third of the spinach leaves. Sprinkle one third of the goat cheese over the spinach, and then one third of the salt and pepper.

Repeat the process twice more, finishing with a fourth layer of potato. Press the sweet potato layers down to compact the spinach. As the gratin cooks, the spinach will wilt and flatten.

Drizzle the remaining garlic oil over the top layer of sweet potato. You should have four layers of sweet potato and three layers of spinach and cheese.

Cover with foil and bake for 20 minutes. Uncover and bake for 30 minutes longer. Test for doneness by inserting a knife into the middle of the gratin. There should be no resistance and the knife should come out smoothly. Serve immediately.

SERVES 4 TO 6

2 large sweet potatoes (about 1½ lbs/750 g total)

2 large cloves garlic, grated

¼ cup extra-virgin olive oil

4 cups packed spinach leaves (about 4 oz/125 g)

1 cup crumbled goat cheese (about 5 oz/150 g)

1 tsp kosher salt

¼ tsp freshly ground black pepper

Do I eat dessert every day? No, but when I do,
I want it to be special. And although Devin is the
pastry guru in our family, I do have a repertoire
of simpler desserts up my sleeve.

LINDA

SWEET THINGS

In this chapter, Mom and I do a switch-up.
I happen to be the dessert expert in the family,
so you may find some of my recipes a bit
more challenging than hers. I figure if I have
the time to make dessert in the first place,
I have time to make a really good one.

DEVIN

Linda

CHOCOLATE PHYLLO TARTS
with ROASTED STRAWBERRY ICE CREAM

Storebought phyllo pastry and Devin's chocolate butter are the secret ingredients in these pretty and delicious little tarts. The rich, creamy chocolate butter is encased in layers of phyllo, then baked just until the tarts turn a beautiful golden color and the chocolate has melted. The roasted strawberry ice cream is a special touch. This recipe will leave you ice cream to spare, but if you're pressed for time or don't have an ice-cream maker, a good-quality storebought strawberry ice cream will do. Both the ice cream and tarts can be made a day ahead. Just reheat the tarts in a 350°F oven for 10 minutes before serving.

SERVES 4

ROASTED STRAWBERRY ICE CREAM

4 cups fresh strawberries (2 pints), hulled

2 tsp balsamic vinegar

¼ tsp freshly ground black pepper

2½ cups 10% (half-and-half) cream

1 cup superfine sugar

TARTS

4 sheets phyllo pastry

¼ cup unsalted clarified butter, melted

½ cup granulated sugar, approx.

¾ cup chocolate butter (page 127), cold

1 tsp Dutch process cocoa powder, for dusting tarts

12 fresh strawberries

Preheat the oven to 400°F.

For the ice cream, toss together the berries, vinegar and pepper in a baking dish. Roast for about 15 minutes, or until the strawberries are soft but still hold their shape. Remove from the oven and cool in the dish for 10 minutes.

Meanwhile, whisk together the cream and superfine sugar in a large bowl.

Puree the warm berries and stir into the cream. It is important that the berries be warm (heat them slightly if they have cooled) to melt the sugar.

Cover and refrigerate for at least 1 hour. Place the strawberry mixture in an ice-cream maker and follow the manufacturer's instructions.

Scoop the ice cream into a container and freeze until serving.

Meanwhile, for the tart, cut the sheets of phyllo into 12-inch squares (discard the edges). Cover with waxed paper or parchment paper and a tea towel to prevent them from drying out. (The remaining phyllo can be refrozen or stored, tightly wrapped, in the refrigerator for up to 4 days.)

Cut the phyllo squares into quarters. Keeping the remaining phyllo covered, lightly brush one square with melted butter. Sprinkle with 1 tsp sugar. Place another sheet of phyllo on top and repeat with the butter and sugar. Continue with the remaining layers, omitting the butter and sugar from the fourth layer.

Repeat with the remaining squares of phyllo.

Place 3 Tbsp chilled chocolate butter in the center of each stack of phyllo and brush melted butter around the edge. Press the stacks into four lightly greased ½-cup muffin cups.

Pull the four corners of the phyllo over the chocolate, twisting the tops to form a rose-like top. Brush the tarts lightly with melted butter, being sure to get into all the crevices. Sprinkle the tops with 1 to 2 tsp granulated sugar and refrigerate for 30 minutes. Fill any empty muffin cups with a little water.

Place the muffin pan on a baking sheet and bake for 8 to 10 minutes, or until the phyllo is golden brown.

Place the tarts on serving plates and let sit for about 5 minutes to allow the chocolate to cool slightly. Dust with sifted cocoa and serve with the ice cream and fresh strawberries.

KITCHEN HINTS

CLARIFIED BUTTER

To clarify butter, melt butter over low heat until a white froth appears on top of the fat. Strain the liquid through a fine sieve (you may have to do this three or four times) until all the froth has been removed. You will lose about 20 percent of the volume.

SUPERFINE SUGAR

Superfine sugar (also called castor sugar or bar sugar) is simply finely ground granulated sugar. It dissolves more easily than regular sugar. You can buy it or make your own. For 1 cup superfine sugar, place 1 cup plus 1 tsp regular granulated sugar in a food processor and pulse until finely ground.

MAKES ONE 9-INCH SQUARE
OR 11-INCH ROUND TART

TART SHELL

1½ cups unbleached all-purpose flour

½ cup Dutch process cocoa powder

3 Tbsp granulated sugar

¼ tsp kosher salt

¾ cup unsalted butter, cold, cut in
    ½-inch cubes

1 large egg yolk

3 Tbsp cold water

FILLING

1 cup 35% (whipping) cream

½ cup whole milk

¼ tsp kosher salt

8 oz (250 g) semisweet chocolate,
    roughly chopped

2 oz (60 g) bittersweet chocolate,
    roughly chopped

2 large eggs, at room temperature,
    lightly beaten

2 Tbsp sifted confectioners' (icing)
    sugar, or cocoa, for dusting

DECADENT DARK CHOCOLATE TART
(photo page 198)

I learned the basics of this recipe when I spent a summer at the Cordon Bleu in Paris. While I usually like to make a dish in the simplest and quickest way possible, I always spend lots of time on dessert. I learned early on that you can't rush pastry or desserts anyway, so you kind of have to just get in the zone and stick with it.

This particular tart is so creamy and delicious, and it is perfect when served at room temperature. This is my Valentine's Day special because it evokes lots of mmmmming and ooooohing, and that's even before you taste it. I promise you that this recipe will not disappoint.

Chocolate lover's alert: This tart is for the dark chocolate aficionado (and make sure you use good-quality chocolate). You will probably only need a sliver to leave you satisfied.

For the tart shell, combine the flour, cocoa, granulated sugar and salt in a food processor.

Add the butter to the flour mixture, pulsing on/off until the butter is the size of peas.

Whisk the egg yolk and cold water together in a small bowl. Slowly add this to the food processor, pulsing on/off until the dough looks moist but has not yet formed a solid mass. (Test the dough. A large pinch should come together. If it is still crumbly, add 1 to 2 Tbsp water and process briefly.)

Remove the dough from the food processor and press together, forming it into a disk 1 inch thick. Cover with plastic wrap and refrigerate for 1 hour.

Remove the plastic wrap and roll the chilled dough into a large circle between 2 sheets of parchment paper or plastic wrap until it is ⅛ inch thick. (This is where things can get tricky because the pastry is very delicate. If it starts to crack or fall apart, just press the pieces back together with your fingers.)

Carefully transfer the pastry to a 9-inch square or 11-inch round tart pan with a removable bottom. Press the pastry into the pan, paying close attention to the scalloped edges. Remove any extra dough by pressing it off with your fingers. If the dough tears, just patch the holes with some of the extra pastry. You will have some pastry left over. If you wish, cut it into shapes, sprinkle with granulated sugar and bake for 15 minutes.

Refrigerate the tart shell in the pan for 15 to 30 minutes. Prick the bottom of the uncooked pastry several times with a fork.

Preheat the oven to 375°F.

Line the bottom of the tart shell with parchment and weigh down with dried beans or rice to prevent the pastry from puffing up while you blind bake it.

Bake the tart shell for 15 minutes. Remove the parchment and the dried beans and continue to bake for 5 minutes. Allow the tart shell to rest on a wire rack while you make the filling.

For the filling, heat the cream and milk in a saucepan over medium heat until the edges of the liquid just begin to simmer.

Remove the pan from the heat and stir in the salt and chopped chocolate until completely melted. Stir in the beaten eggs.

Pour the chocolate filling into the cooled tart shell and smooth the surface with a spatula. Bake for about 20 minutes, or until the filling is just set (not wobbly) when you shake the pan gently. If you see any cracking, remove the tart from the oven immediately. The final tart should be smooth and shiny. Allow to cool for at least 2 hours before serving. Dust the top with sifted icing sugar.

KITCHEN HINT

PASTRY 101

- Sometimes pastry can fall apart when you are transferring it from the counter to the tart tin. Don't worry about this too much, as you can always patch cracks or holes with extra bits of pastry. It might not look perfect, but once the tart is baked and filled, you won't even notice the difference.
- Before baking, refrigerate your pastry. This will relax the glutens in the flour, which prevents shrinking.
- Blind baking means baking a pie crust without the filling. Sometimes blind baking means partially cooked and sometimes completely.

Linda

1 cup soda water

1 cup dry white wine

3 Tbsp granulated sugar

1 strip lemon zest, ½ inch by 2 inches,
    preferably organic

1 strip orange zest, ½ inch by 2 inches,
    preferably organic

10 raspberries, plus extra for garnish

5 fresh mint leaves, plus extra for
    garnish

4 ripe peaches

4 scoops vanilla yogurt gelato
    (page 209) or vanilla or
    lemon frozen yogurt

PEACHES STEEPED IN WHITE WINE, RASPBERRY *and* MINT *with* VANILLA YOGURT GELATO

You will want to make this sophisticated, light, fresh-tasting dessert in the summer months when peaches are at their peak. It will take you 15 minutes to prepare and can be made hours ahead. Poaching a few raspberries in the liquid turns it a pale rose color — a beautiful contrast to the golden slices of peach.

Combine the soda water, wine, sugar, lemon and orange zest, raspberries and mint in a saucepan and bring to a low boil. Reduce the heat and simmer for 8 minutes.

Meanwhile, bring a large pot of water to a boil. Plunge the peaches into the boiling water for 30 to 45 seconds to loosen their skins. Cool the peaches in cold water. Peel, cut into ½-inch wedges and place in a heatproof bowl.

Pour the hot liquid over the fruit and let them infuse for 3 to 4 hours. The peaches should be served at room temperature but can be refrigerated for a few hours if you want to make them ahead.

Arrange the peaches in a windmill pattern in individual shallow bowls. Place a scoop of gelato in the center of each serving and garnish with a few fresh raspberries and mint leaves.

Devin

RASPBERRY, BLACKBERRY
and PROSECCO MINT JELLY

SERVES 8

GELATIN MIXTURE
2 Tbsp unflavored gelatin powder
   (2 packages)

½ cup warm water

JELLY
1 cup water

⅓ cup granulated sugar

1 Tbsp lightly packed grated orange
   zest (about 1 medium), preferably
   organic

3 cups Prosecco or other sparkling
   white wine (750 mL bottle)

1 generous cup raspberries
   (about 6 oz/175 g)

1 generous cup blackberries
   (about 6 oz/175 g)

1 Tbsp lightly packed finely chopped
   fresh mint

This is a very sophisticated version of those evil neon-colored Jell-O shooters that we've probably all had unpleasant experiences with. I love serving these at parties because they are really beautiful when cut into squares and served on Chinese soup spoons. You can also scoop the jelly out and pile it into Champagne or wine glasses to be eaten with a spoon. I adore the faint hint of the Prosecco bubbles scented with the orange zest.

P.S. You probably don't want to serve these to the kiddies, because I don't boil the mixture to cook off the alcohol.

Combine the gelatin and warm water in a small bowl.

Combine 1 cup water, the sugar and orange zest in a large saucepan and bring to a low boil over medium-low heat to dissolve the sugar.

Remove from the heat and stir in the gelatin mixture.

Gently pour in the Prosecco and stir lightly.

Ladle the liquid into a 13- by 9-inch baking dish. The liquid should be about an inch deep.

Scatter the berries and mint evenly over the liquid. If the berries float, push them down with your finger.

Refrigerate for 4 to 5 hours, or until set. Cut into squares or scoop into glasses.

Linda

HAZELNUT MERINGUE MILLEFEUILLES *with* WHIPPED CREAM *and* SUMMER BERRIES

My husband has a soft spot for meringue, and my mother had a passion for the French pastry millefeuille. I was able to gain a lot of points with both of them when I made this for dessert. Even a meringue-baking novice will have no trouble getting this right. The meringue is simply spread on a baking sheet — no need for piping bags and steady hands. It can be made up to two days ahead. Cut it into pieces and store in an airtight container.

Feel free to change the nuts and fruit, depending on what's in season. Almonds and peaches or plums and pistachios are delicious combinations. I have also switched up the whipped cream with softened ice cream in the summer.

You can assemble the dessert up to an hour and a half before serving.

Preheat the oven to 375°F.

For the meringues, place the hazelnuts on a baking sheet and bake for 5 minutes. While the nuts are still warm, wrap them in a tea towel and rub vigorously until most of the brown skin is removed. Finely chop by hand or in a food processor and set aside (the hazelnuts should still have some texture).

Reduce the oven temperature to 195°F.

Place the egg whites in a large bowl and put the bowl in warm water until the eggs are slightly warmer than room temperature. Add the salt and, using an electric mixer, whip them until they have soft peaks. Add 1 cup granulated sugar a tablespoon at a time and continue to whip until the peaks are stiff and glossy. Fold in the hazelnuts.

Line a baking sheet with parchment paper, using a drop of meringue under each corner to prevent the parchment from curling.

SERVES 4

MERINGUE

1 cup hazelnuts (about 5 oz/150 g)

5 large egg whites

Pinch of kosher salt

1 cup granulated sugar

FILLING

3 cups fresh strawberries, trimmed and cut lengthwise in slices ¼ inch thick, plus halved strawberries (with greens) for garnish

1 Tbsp freshly squeezed lemon juice

2 Tbsp granulated sugar, divided

1½ cups 35% (whipping) cream

1 tsp vanilla extract

1 Tbsp sifted confectioners' (icing) sugar, for dusting

Spread the meringue evenly over the parchment paper to form a 14- by 11-inch rectangle. Bake for 2 hours. The meringue should be barely pale gold. Remove from the oven and transfer the parchment paper to a cutting board. Using a bread knife, immediately trim the edges (your treat to eat) and cut the meringue into 12 equal pieces, 5 by 2 inches. Don't worry if a few of them crack. They can be used for the middle or bottom layer.

For the filling, toss the sliced strawberries, lemon juice and 1 Tbsp granulated sugar in a bowl 30 minutes before assembling the millefeuilles.

Put the cream and vanilla extract in a separate bowl and whip with an electric mixer until slightly thick. Add the remaining 1 Tbsp granulated sugar and continue to whip until the cream mounds and is spreadable.

To assemble the millefeuilles, spread 2 to 3 Tbsp whipped cream over 4 pieces of meringue and layer with strawberries. Continue with another meringue layer. Cover with cream and top with strawberries. Finish with a layer of meringue. Place on plate. Dust with sifted confectioners' sugar and garnish with halved strawberries.

Devin

CHEEKY MONKEY ICE CREAM CAKE

SERVES 10

4 cups (1 L) good-quality vanilla
   ice cream

1 cup smooth peanut butter

2 ripe bananas

1 cup gingersnap cookie crumbs
   (about 18 small cookies,
   or 3 oz/90 g)

Like Mom's millefeuilles, this dessert is made in layers. If you are a fan of peanut butter and banana sandwiches, then this may become your new favorite. (Elvis may rolling over in his grave about missing out on this one.)

To crush the cookies, put them in a heavy-duty plastic bag and crush with a rolling pin, wine bottle or baseball bat (kidding) until they are fine crumbs.

Allow the ice cream to soften for 10 to 15 minutes at room temperature. Line an 8- by 4-inch loaf pan with plastic wrap.

Stir together the softened ice cream and peanut butter in a large bowl until well incorporated.

Spoon a third of the ice cream into the loaf pan, smoothing the top. Bang the pan on the counter a couple of times to remove any air bubbles.

Peel and cut the bananas into rounds ¼ inch thick. Place one layer of overlapping banana slices on top of the ice cream and then top with half the crumbs.

Spoon a third of the ice cream over the crumbs and gently smooth so as not to mix the layer of bananas and crumbs into the ice cream. Top with the remaining crumbs and another layer of banana. Smooth the remaining ice cream over top. Cover with plastic wrap and freeze for at least 4 hours before serving.

Invert the loaf pan on a plate. Heat a dishcloth with hot water and wipe the pan to gently soften the outside layer of ice cream. Pull the plastic wrap to further loosen the cake. You may have to do a bit of wiggling to get it out of the mold. Slice using a sharp knife dipped in hot water.

Linda

BABY PUMPKIN PUDDINGS *with* CINNAMON WHIPPED CREAM *and* PECAN BRITTLE

I have a confession to make. These delicate baby puddings scented with a touch of rum and orange zest started life as the filling for my mother's pumpkin pie. But since I don't have Devin's deft hand in the pastry department, I decided to skip the crust and make these sweet little desserts instead. (Though for Thanksgiving dinner Devin and I work in tandem and turn out a pie that would make Mom proud.)

The puddings can be made a day ahead and refrigerated, but bring them to room temperature before serving.

For the brittle, melt half the sugar in a small heavy saucepan over medium-low heat. Once the sugar starts to melt around the edge of the pan, stir until all the sugar has melted. Add the remaining sugar and stir until it has turned a caramel color. This could take up to 15 minutes. If you have a candy thermometer, it should register 250°F (120°C), just below hard boil.

Stir in the pecans and salt and quickly pour the mixture onto a lightly buttered counter or baking sheet. Use a lightly oiled spatula to smooth the brittle into a thin layer (about ¼ inch thick). Allow to cool and then break into shards. Extra brittle will keep in a closed container for a few days.

Preheat the oven to 350°F.

For the puddings, combine the pumpkin, brown sugar, salt, cinnamon, ginger, nutmeg and mace in a large bowl.

Whisk together the eggs, evaporated milk, rum and orange zest in a separate bowl. Stir the egg mixture into the puree.

Divide the custard among six ¾-cup ovenproof ramekins and place in a roasting pan. If there are any small bubbles on top of

SERVES 6

PECAN BRITTLE
1½ cups granulated sugar

¾ cup pecan halves (about 3 oz/90 g), broken in rough quarters

Pinch of kosher salt

PUDDINGS
14-oz (398 mL) can pumpkin puree (not pumpkin pie filling), about 1¾ cups

¾ cup lightly packed light brown sugar

¾ tsp kosher salt

1 tsp ground cinnamon

½ tsp ground ginger

½ tsp ground nutmeg

¼ tsp ground mace

2 large eggs

1½ cups evaporated milk (not condensed) or 18% cream

2 Tbsp dark rum

½ tsp lightly packed grated orange zest, preferably organic

CINNAMON WHIPPED CREAM
½ cup 35% (whipping) cream

½ tsp vanilla extract

1 tsp granulated sugar

⅛ tsp ground cinnamon

the custards, draw the tip of a small knife across the top to break them.

Make a *bain marie* by pouring warm water into the roasting pan until it comes halfway up the sides of the ramekins. Place a piece of foil lightly over the top and bake for 45 to 50 minutes, or until the puddings are barely quivering in the middle.

Remove the ramekins from the oven, cool on a rack and refrigerate, covered, until an hour before serving.

For the whipped cream, combine the cream and vanilla in a bowl and whip until soft peaks form. Add the sugar and cinnamon. Whip until the cream is soft and billowy. Refrigerate.

Garnish the flans with a dollop of whipped cream and a shard of pecan brittle.

. . . .

KITCHEN HINT

STRONG GRIP: NON-SLIP TONGS
To easily remove ramekins or preserving jars from hot water, wrap elastic bands around the ends of your tongs.

. . . .

Devin

WHIPPED CHEESECAKE MOUSSE *with* CINNAMON GRAHAM CRACKER CRUNCH

SERVES 8

8 oz (250 g) cream cheese,
   at room temperature

2 cups 35% (whipping) cream,
   cold, divided

¼ cup sour cream

¼ cup plus 1 Tbsp granulated sugar

Seeds of ½ vanilla bean, or 1 tsp
   vanilla extract

½ cup Graham cracker crumbs
   (about 6 crackers)

¼ tsp ground cinnamon

1 cup finely chopped fresh
   strawberries (about 14)

8 sprigs of fresh mint, for garnish

My older brother, John, can put away a whole cheesecake in one sitting. It's miraculous — truly. He also happens to clock marathons in under 4 hours. He is the embodiment of checks and balances. (Although I'm sure I could put away a whole cheesecake, you won't see me near a marathon. No checks or balances for me.)

This cheesecake mousse is light, airy, creamy, sweet and tangy all at once. It totally fulfills my craving without me having to mow down on a whole cake. It is also simplicity come to life. No cooking required.

With a mixer on low, beat the cream cheese, ½ cup whipping cream, sour cream, sugar and vanilla in a bowl. Increase the speed to high and beat until light and fluffy, about 3 minutes.

In a separate large bowl with clean beaters, beat the remaining 1½ cups whipping cream on high until stiff peaks form.

Stir a large spoonful of the whipped cream into the cream cheese mixture to lighten its texture.

Add the cream cheese mixture back to the remaining whipped cream and gently fold in to thoroughly combine.

Combine the Graham cracker crumbs and cinnamon in a small bowl.

Using 8 Moroccan tea glasses or small delicate glasses (about ⅔ cup each), place ½ Tbsp Graham cracker crumbs in the bottom of each glass. Top with a layer of mousse to fill half of the glass. Add a layer of chopped strawberries and then another layer of mousse to the top of the glass. Top with the remaining crumbs, some chopped strawberries, and a sprig of mint.

Refrigerate for 1 hour before serving.

SERVES 6

6 medium oranges

2 Tbsp white Lillet,
   Pineau des Charentes
   or orange-flavored liqueur

¼ cup pomegranate seeds

4 to 6 fresh mint leaves,
   roughly ripped

Linda

CHILLED ORANGE, POMEGRANATE *and* MINT CARPACCIO

This is my standby dessert when time is of the essence. If pomegranates are out of season, sprinkle the oranges with raspberries, and if kids are going to partake, substitute a couple of tablespoons of orange juice for the liqueur. Oatmeal cookies (page 194) or shortbread (page 195) are great accompaniments.

Cut a thin slice off the top and bottom of the oranges. Rest a flat surface of the fruit on a chopping board. Following the contour of the orange, slice away the rind and pith from top to bottom. Cut each orange into ¼-inch slices.

Arrange the orange slices overlapping on a serving dish (I use a large round platter). Sprinkle with Lillet. Chill.

Top the oranges with the pomegranate seeds and mint.
Serve cool but not cold.

· ·

KITCHEN HINT

LILLET AND PINEAU DES CHARENTES

Lillet is an aperitif from the Bordeaux region of France. It can be red or white, although the white version is more readily available. It is shimmery golden in color with a scent of honey and candied orange, but without an overpowering sweet taste.

Pineau des Charentes is similar to Lillet but a bit heavier and sweeter. It is made from a blend of unfermented grape must and Cognac, making it a vin de liqueur. Serve both cool in sherry glasses.

· ·

Devin

ROASTED BROWN SUGAR PEARS
ON CINNAMON TOAST BRUSCHETTA

This recipe is shockingly good and shockingly simple. Like my mom's dessert carpaccio it is one of my favorite recipes when I have a time limit but want to impress. I love caramelized pears, and paired with crisp, warm cinnamon toast, it doesn't get much better. Serve this bruschetta (and FYI it's "broos-KEH-tah," not "broo-SHEH-tah") with vanilla ice cream for a special treat.

Preheat the oven to 400°F.

Cut each pear in half lengthwise and remove the core with a teaspoon.

Rub all sides of the pears with the butter and place cut side down on a parchment- or foil-lined baking sheet.

Sprinkle the pears with the brown sugar and bake for 15 minutes.

Meanwhile, for the bruschetta, combine the butter, brown sugar, cinnamon and cardamom in a small bowl.

Heat a grill pan over high heat. Grill the bread for about 2 minutes on each side, until charred grill marks form (if you don't have a grill pan, just toast the bread).

While the toast is still hot, spread the spiced butter over each piece.

Remove the pears from the oven and slice each section in half, placing two pieces on each piece of toast.

SERVES 4

ROASTED PEARS
2 Bosc pears

½ Tbsp unsalted butter,
    at room temperature

1 Tbsp light brown sugar

CINNAMON TOAST BRUSCHETTA
3 Tbsp unsalted butter,
    at room temperature

1½ Tbsp light brown sugar

½ tsp ground cinnamon

½ tsp ground cardamom

4 slices white Italian bread,
    about 1 inch thick

Linda

MOM'S OATMEAL COOKIES

1 cup unsalted butter, at room
  temperature

1 cup granulated sugar

1 cup lightly packed light brown sugar

1 large egg

1½ cups unbleached all-purpose flour

1 tsp baking powder

1 tsp baking soda

1 cup desiccated sweetened coconut

1 cup quick-cooking rolled oats
  (not instant)

Although my mom didn't often make desserts, she made this cookie on a regular basis. It was my dad's favorite, and after Martin and I married, it became his favorite, too. The cookies stay fresh for up to four days in a cookie jar. They also freeze beautifully (although we haven't had to worry about that in our house).

Preheat the oven to 350°F.

Cream together the butter, sugars and egg in a large bowl.

Combine the flour, baking powder and baking soda in a separate bowl. Stir the flour mixture into the eggs.

Mix half the coconut and rolled oats into the dough to combine. Mix in the remaining coconut and rolled oats.

Drop 1 Tbsp balls of dough onto lightly buttered baking sheets and flatten with a fork until about ⅛ inch thick, creating a crosshatch pattern. Leave about 1 inch between cookies. Dip the fork in a glass of cold water occasionally to prevent the dough from sticking to it.

Bake the cookies for 12 to 18 minutes, or until golden brown. Cool on a baking rack.

BEAUTY TIP

Don't-Eat-That-Oatmeal
Beauty Scrub

In a bowl, combine 2 Tbsp rolled oats and 2 Tbsp cornmeal. Stir in 1 Tbsp honey to make a paste. Peel and chop half a small tart apple.

In a food processor, combine the apple and paste and pulse until the mixture is well blended.

Spread the mixture on your face and gently scrub in a circular motion to remove dead skin cells. Rinse with lukewarm water and apply your favorite mask.

Makes enough scrub for you and a friend.

Devin

SUGAR *and* SPICE SHORTBREAD

Living in London, I became quite partial to my four o'clock cup of tea with bickies. My office friends and I would take turns doing the tea rounds and would usually end up sharing a crummy Kit Kat bar. These sugary cinnamon bites would have been a much nicer accompaniment.

This is one of those amazing recipes that fills your house (or one-bedroom apartment) with a blissfully sweet aroma. Often I roll the dough into a log, cover it with plastic wrap and throw it in the freezer to bake off whenever I want.

Combine the flour, allspice and salt in a bowl.

Using an electric mixer on medium, beat the butter in a large bowl for 1 minute. Add the confectioners' sugar and vanilla. Increase the speed to high and beat for 4 minutes. Reduce the speed to low and mix in the flour mixture until just combined.

Form the dough into a ball and place it on a sheet of plastic wrap. Flatten the disk until it is about 1 inch thick and wrap tightly. Refrigerate for 15 minutes.

Roll out the dough on a lightly floured surface until it is ½ inch thick. Using a 1½-inch round cookie cutter, cut out as many cookies as possible and place ½ inch apart on parchment-lined baking sheets. You should have about 40 cookies. Refrigerate the cookies for at least 15 minutes.

Preheat the oven to 325°F.

Prick each cookie twice with a fork. Combine the sugar and cinnamon in a small bowl and sprinkle it evenly over the cookies.

Bake for 25 minutes, or until lightly golden (you will probably have to bake them in batches). Remove the cookies from the baking sheet and cool on a wire rack for 20 minutes before storing in an airtight container.

MAKES ABOUT 40 COOKIES

DOUGH

2¼ cups unbleached all-purpose flour

2½ tsp ground allspice

⅛ tsp kosher salt

1½ cups unsalted butter,
   at room temperature

1 cup confectioners' (icing) sugar

1 tsp vanilla extract

TOPPING

3 Tbsp granulated sugar

1 tsp ground cinnamon

LUCY'S ALMOND TART

Lucy Alves, who was born in Portugal, was my mother's devoted caregiver. She would make this beautiful tart on a regular basis and, if we were lucky, she would send us home with one. The base has a shortbread texture, and in the summer Lucy fills it with whipped cream and berries. In cold weather I serve this with fruit compote and a dollop of whipped cream. It will stay fresh on your counter for two to three days and can be frozen for up to two months.

For the crust, combine the flour and sugar in a large bowl. Add the butter and crumble the mixture with your fingertips until it has the texture of coarse cornmeal.

Add three-quarters of the beaten eggs and mix them in with your hands until the dough holds together. Add the remaining egg if necessary. The dough will be sticky. Pat the dough into an 8- to 9-inch disk, wrap in plastic wrap and refrigerate for 30 minutes.

Unwrap the dough and use your fingers to press the dough evenly into the bottom and sides of a 10-inch tart pan with a removable bottom. Freeze for 30 minutes.

Preheat the oven to 350°F.

Prick the base of the tart several times with a fork and bake for 20 minutes. (The edges of the tart may slip down the sides of the pan, but don't panic. Once you add the topping the sides will rise around it.)

Meanwhile, for the topping, melt the butter, sugar and milk in a small saucepan, stirring occasionally. Bring to a rolling boil for 2 minutes. Add the almonds and continue to boil for another 2 minutes. The mixture should be a little creamy and light beige in color. Remove from the heat and immediately pour into the warm crust, spreading it evenly with a spatula.

MAKES ONE 10-INCH TART

CRUST

1¾ cups plus 2 Tbsp unbleached all-purpose flour

1½ cups granulated sugar

¾ cup unsalted butter, cold, cut in small cubes

2 large eggs, lightly beaten

TOPPING

½ cup plus 1 Tbsp unsalted butter, cold

½ cup granulated sugar

6 Tbsp whole milk

1¼ cups slivered almonds (about 5½ oz/160 g)

Place the tart on a foil-lined baking sheet to catch any spills and bake for about 25 minutes, or until the tart is dark golden. Cool for 15 minutes before removing from the pan.

DRUNKEN FRUIT COMPOTE

Wrap a broken cinnamon stick and 16 black peppercorns in cheesecloth.

Combine 1 cup water, 1 cup ruby port and 1 Tbsp maple syrup in a large saucepan and bring to a simmer. Add the sachet of spices, 1 cup prunes, ½ cup sliced dried apples, 1 cup halved dried apricots and a ½- by 3-inch strip of orange zest.

Return to a simmer and cook for 10 to 15 minutes, or until the liquid has become slightly syrupy and the fruit has plumped. Remove the sachet and orange zest and transfer the compote to a serving bowl. Sprinkle with 1 tsp grated lemon zest.

This will keep for up to a week and can also be served warm over porridge or vanilla or caramel ice cream.

Makes 4 to 5 cups.

ORANGE THYME INFUSION

After a decadent mid-afternoon tasting of fabulous cheeses that Devin and I had bought at our favorite fromagerie in Paris, we brewed up this pale orange infusion at our rental apartment. We mixed thyme (an herb that aids digestion) with the sparkle of orange, making it possible for us to meet friends for dinner at a local bistro a few hours later.

Peel an orange with a vegetable peeler (use only the peel, not the pith) and place the peel and a large sprig of fresh thyme in a tea pot.

Pour in 3 cups boiling water and let steep for 5 minutes.

Makes 3 cups.

Devin

FRESH FIG TART ON HAZELNUT CRUST
with CRUNCHY CARAMEL CROWN

I first made this recipe in Paris after buying freshly roasted hazelnuts, unpasteurized crème fraîche and sticky ripe figs at an out-
door market on the Right Bank. The second time I made it was for
lunch with the lovely Chuck Williams (founder of Williams-
Sonoma). He loved it so much that he had a second piece and then
took the rest home with him. That's when I knew the recipe had to
be included in this book!

I have divided the recipe into stages so, if you prefer, you can
make all the components ahead of time and assemble them at the
last minute. The crunchy caramel "crown" on the tart will stay hard
for up to an hour once assembled.

I like to use Black Mission figs in this tart for the best color and
flavor, although you can use any fresh green or purple figs.

For the tart shell, toast the hazelnuts in a dry skillet over
medium-high heat for 6 to 7 minutes, stirring constantly.
The skins should start to darken and crack and there should
be a noticeable aroma.

Wrap the nuts in a clean tea towel and vigorously rub them
together to separate the skin from the nuts. You will not be able
to remove all of the skin, which is fine. Place the nuts in a sieve
and shake to remove any extra skin.

Place the skinned nuts in a food processor with ¼ cup granulated
sugar. Pulse the nuts and sugar until they become a fine powder.
Be careful not to overprocess the nuts, as they can turn into
hazelnut butter.

In a bowl, use a fork to mix together the hazelnut and sugar
mixture with the flour and melted butter. The dough should
have a granular texture and stick together when pinched.

Spoon the dough out into a 9-inch fluted tart pan with a
removable bottom and press it out with your fingers until

MAKES ONE 9-INCH TART

¾ cup hazelnuts

½ cup granulated sugar, divided

½ cup unbleached all-purpose flour

¼ cup unsalted butter, melted

1 cup crème fraîche (page 201)

½ Tbsp lightly packed grated
    orange zest (about ½ medium),
    preferably organic

18 large ripe purple figs

KITCHEN HINT

FIG FACTS

Figs date back to 3000 B.C. and were used by the Assyrians as sweeteners. They were also said to be the favorite fruit of Cleopatra. Dark purple Black Mission figs are in season from June to September. They have an intense, sweet flavor, beautiful color and soft, thin skins. Look for figs that are soft to the touch but not mushy, and that are free of nicks and bruises. Fresh figs are fragile, but they can be stored in the refrigerator for a day or two.

it forms a uniform layer ¼ inch thick on the bottom and sides of the pan. Refrigerate for 30 minutes.

Preheat the oven to 350°F.

Remove the crust from the fridge and prick the surface several times with a fork.

Because the filling for the tart is uncooked, you must blind bake the tart. To do this, line the chilled pastry with a sheet of parchment and top with an even layer of pastry weights (dried beans or rice work very well). This will prevent the pastry from rising while it bakes.

Bake the tart shell for 15 minutes.

Carefully remove the parchment and the weights and return the tart to the oven for another 15 minutes. The pastry should be firm to the touch and a light golden brown. Allow the tart to cool completely before filling it.

For the caramel strands, heat the remaining ¼ cup granulated sugar in a small saucepan over medium heat. Resist stirring for the first 3 minutes, then stir the sugar until it is completely melted and a medium caramel color. Be careful not to burn the mixture. (It will start to smoke if it is burning.) Remove the caramel from the heat and allow it to cool for about 2 minutes. When the caramel is removed from the stove, it is too thin to drizzle immediately. It must cool and thicken slightly before it will form thin strands.

To test the caramel, dip in a fork and pull it out to see if the caramel forms long thin strands. When it is the right consistency, drizzle the caramel onto a sheet of parchment paper in a circular shape roughly the same diameter as the tart. Fill in the circle in a swirly spider web pattern so that when it hardens it will hold together in one piece. Allow the caramel to cool until hard.

For the filling, combine the crème fraîche and orange zest in a bowl. Spread an even layer over the bottom of the pastry shell.

Remove the hard-stemmed tips of the figs and cut them lengthwise into slices ¼ inch thick. You should get 5 to 6 slices from each fig.

Create a concentric circle pattern by overlapping the fig slices until you reach the center of the tart.

Gently peel the parchment paper away from the hardened caramel crown and place it on the tart. Serve immediately. The tart will hold at room temperature for just under an hour before the caramel begins to soften.

CRÈME FRAÎCHE

If your local store doesn't carry crème fraîche, here is my foolproof recipe for making your own.

Whisk together 1 cup 35% (whipping) cream and ¼ cup buttermilk in a bowl. Lightly cover with a tea towel and leave at room temperature for 12 to 24 hours, or until the mixture is the consistency of lightly whipped cream. Cover and refrigerate until ready to use.

Crème fraîche should keep in the refrigerator for up to a week. It can be used as a substitute for sour cream in some recipes.

Linda

RHUBARB PISTACHIO CRUMBLE

⅔ cup shelled pistachios, coarsely
chopped (about 3 oz/90 g)

1 cup quick-cooking (not instant)
rolled oats

⅔ cup unbleached all-purpose flour

½ cup firmly packed light brown sugar

⅔ cup unsalted butter, ice cold,
cut in ¼-inch cubes

7 cups rhubarb, trimmed and cut in
1-inch pieces (about 2½ lbs/1 kg)

3 Tbsp instant tapioca

2 tsp lightly packed grated lime zest,
preferably organic

1¼ to 1⅓ cups granulated sugar
(depending on sourness of rhubarb)

Even I can make Devin's foolproof cream cheese pastry, so in autumn her apple tarts (page 205) become my mainstay dessert. But in spring when the first rhubarb lands in the markets, I gravitate toward this easy homey crumble. The pistachios in the crumble and the slight citrus boost in the fruit make an old-fashioned favorite a little more sophisticated.

Serve it warm with sweetened yogurt or crème fraîche (page 201) or a scoop of vanilla gelato (page 209).

Preheat the oven to 350°F.

Combine the nuts, rolled oats, flour and brown sugar in a bowl. Add the butter and combine with your hands (cold hands, please), pinching or smearing the butter into the other ingredients with the heel of your hand until large, moist clumps form. The trick is not to take it too far. You don't want the butter to be completely softened.

Toss the rhubarb, tapioca, lime zest and granulated sugar together in a large bowl. Spread in a 10-cup shallow baking dish and cover with the crumble mixture. Place on a baking sheet (as this loves to bubble up) and bake for about 1¼ hours, or until the top is golden. Serve slightly warm or at room temperature.

Devin

PETITES TARTES AUX POMMES
with CALVADOS CRÈME ANGLAISE

If there is something about making apple pie that encourages you to feel virtuous and wholesome, then these delectable little wonders will do your soul some good. The crème anglaise is a perfect match for the warm tarts. It can be made up to two days ahead and is best served chilled to counterbalance the hot pies.

Be prepared to become a pastry chef with this recipe. You will be able to boast to your friends that you can now make a beautiful flaky pastry from scratch. What you don't have to tell them is that you did it with three ingredients, in one bowl and in 5 minutes.

For any pie, tart or cookie, this is the easiest and most delicious pastry ever.

For the pastry, combine the flour, salt, butter and cream cheese in a large bowl. Pinch the butter and cream cheese between your fingers until they form moist clumps. This should take about 3 to 4 minutes. Give the dough one or two extra kneads and press it into a ball. Work the pastry as little as possible to prevent it from becoming tough.

Place the ball of dough on a sheet of plastic wrap and press to form a disk about 1 inch thick. Cover with another sheet of plastic wrap and refrigerate for at least 1 hour.

When ready to use, place the pastry disk between 2 sheets of parchment or waxed paper and roll out until ⅛ inch thick.

Using a paring knife or cookie cutter, cut out six 5-inch and six 3-inch circles. Don't worry about making perfect circles (it just adds to the rustic appearance). Form any leftover dough scraps into a ball and reroll it to make more circles, if needed. (You will have a little extra dough left over. If you like, cut it into irregular shapes, sprinkle with sugar and bake to make little sugar cookies.)

MAKES 6 TARTS

CREAM CHEESE PASTRY

1¾ cups unbleached all-purpose flour

Pinch of kosher salt

1 cup unsalted butter, cold, cut in ½-inch cubes

1 cup (8 oz/250 g) cream cheese, cold, cut in ½-inch cubes

FILLING

2 Tbsp unsalted butter

6 Golden Delicious apples, peeled, cored and cut in 1-inch chunks

1½ tsp vanilla extract

2 Tbsp freshly squeezed lemon juice (about ½ medium)

¼ cup light brown sugar

¼ tsp ground cinnamon

1 large egg

1 Tbsp granulated sugar

Calvados Crème Anglaise (page 207)

Press the larger pastry circles into six ½-cup muffin cups, making sure to remove any air pockets between the pastry and the sides of the cup. You will have to fold and overlap the pastry, but that's fine. Refrigerate.

For the filling, melt the butter in a large skillet over high heat until it begins to brown. Add the apples, vanilla and lemon juice and stir. Cook for 5 minutes, stirring once or twice to allow some browning.

Add the brown sugar and cinnamon and cook for 1 minute, or until the sugar has melted and coated the apples. Remove from the heat and transfer to a bowl to cool completely.

Preheat the oven to 375°F.

Fill each pastry-lined muffin cup with the apple filling to form a nice high rounded mound.

Top each pie with the remaining 3-inch pastry circles, pinching the top and bottom edges to form a tight seal around the apple filling.

With a sharp paring knife, cut 3 small slits in the top of each tart to allow the steam to escape while baking.

Whisk the egg in a small bowl and brush on each pastry top. Sprinkle with the granulated sugar.

Bake for 20 to 25 minutes, or until golden brown and bubbling. Remove from the oven and allow the tarts to cool in the pan for 10 minutes on a wire rack. Gently wiggle the tarts out of the molds with your hands.

Serve warm with the crème anglaise.

CALVADOS CRÈME ANGLAISE

If you wish, you can replace the Calvados with an extra teaspoon of vanilla extract.

Combine 1¾ cups whole milk, 1 tsp vanilla and 2 Tbsp Calvados in a saucepan. Bring to a simmer over low heat. Immediately remove from the heat and set aside.

Whisk together 4 large egg yolks and ½ cup granulated sugar in a large bowl.

Very slowly pour ¼ cup hot milk into the egg yolk and sugar mixture, whisking vigorously. This will temper the eggs and prevent them from scrambling. Slowly whisk in the rest of the hot milk.

Return the mixture to the saucepan. Stirring constantly with a wooden spoon, cook over medium-low heat for 7 to 9 minutes, or until the mixture has thickened slightly but is still pourable. (To test for doneness, lift the spoon out of the mixture and draw a line down the back of the spoon with your finger. The line should not fill in.)

Remove the pan from the heat and place it in a large bowl of ice. When the custard reaches room temperature, transfer it to a bowl and press a piece of plastic wrap onto the surface to prevent a skin from forming. Refrigerate for at least 30 minutes before serving.

Makes about 2 cups.

Linda

ORANGE CARDAMOM POUND CAKE

MAKES ONE 8- BY-4-INCH CAKE

SYRUP

½ cup granulated sugar

1 cup water

1 cinnamon stick

6 green cardamom pods, lightly crushed with the back of a large knife

2 orange slices, about ¼ inch thick (grate the orange first to get the zest for the cake)

POUND CAKE

1½ cups unbleached all-purpose flour

1 tsp ground cardamom

½ tsp baking soda

Large pinch of kosher salt

½ cup unsalted butter, slightly cooler than room temperature

1 cup plus 2 Tbsp granulated sugar

3 large eggs, divided

3 Tbsp lightly packed grated orange zest (about 3 medium), preferably organic

⅓ cup whole milk yogurt

Although my ability to turn out a perfect pie crust or charming fairy cakes will never match Devin's, I have mastered the mystery of pound cake. The trick is the beaten egg whites—which lighten the dense batter, adding a touch of airiness—and not-too-soft butter. You will have more syrup than you need for the cake; it can be drizzled over fruit salads.

This is also delicious with vanilla yogurt gelato.

For the syrup, combine the sugar, water, cinnamon stick, cardamom pods and orange slices in a small saucepan. Place over medium-high heat and bring to a simmer, cooking until the sugar has dissolved, about 1 minute. Remove from the heat and let rest for at least 1 hour. Strain.

Preheat the oven to 350°F.

For the cake, in a bowl, sift together the flour, cardamom, baking soda and salt.

In a large bowl, cream the butter and sugar with an electric mixer for 4 minutes, or until pale and fluffy.

Lightly beat 1 whole egg, 2 egg yolks and the grated orange zest in a small bowl. Slowly pour this egg mixture into the butter mixture, mixing continuously with an electric mixer until the eggs are just incorporated.

Mix half the flour mixture into the eggs. Follow with half the yogurt, the last of the flour and then the last of the yogurt.

Clean your beaters and whip the egg whites in a bowl just until they form stiff peaks. Gently fold the beaten egg whites into the batter in two additions.

Pour the batter into a lightly buttered and floured 8- by 4-inch loaf pan and bake for 55 minutes, or until a cake tester comes out clean. Remove from the oven and let the cake sit in the pan for 10 minutes before removing to a rack.

Using a cake tester or skewer, poke 12 to 16 holes three-quarters of the way through the cake. Slowly drizzle the syrup over the top (you probably won't use all the syrup).

VANILLA YOGURT GELATO

Line a large fine sieve with a layer of cheesecloth. Balance the sieve over a bowl deep enough to leave about 3 inches between the bottom of the sieve and the bottom of the bowl. Put 6 cups whole-milk yogurt in the sieve and cover with the excess cheesecloth. Refrigerate for 3 hours. You will see a watery liquid in the bottom of the bowl.

Spoon the drained yogurt into a separate bowl. Slice a vanilla bean lengthwise and scrape the seeds out of the pod with the back of a paring knife. Add the vanilla seeds (you could use 2 tsp vanilla extract instead of the seeds), ¼ cup plus 1 Tbsp mild honey and 2 Tbsp light corn syrup to the yogurt and whisk thoroughly. Cover and refrigerate for 1 hour.

Pour the yogurt into an ice-cream maker and follow the manufacturer's instructions. Taste the gelato when it begins to harden. Stir in 1 tsp honey if needed and continue the freezing process. (The gelato will stay frozen without crystallizing due to the addition of the corn syrup.)

Makes 5 generous cups.

CARDAMOM CURRICULUM VITAE

True cardamom seeds, found inside the pods, have a eucalyptus-like scent that fades when the spice is ground. Part of the ginger family, until the 1900s it was grown only in southwest India, but in the past century Guatemala has become the largest producer. Don't substitute black cardamom seeds for green ones. Their taste is very different. Green cardamom has a reputation for improving digestion, detoxifying caffeine and acting as an aphrodisiac.

1 cup whole milk

4 Darjeeling, English Breakfast
   or Orange Pekoe tea bags

2 cups cake flour, sifted

2 tsp baking powder

⅔ cup unsalted butter, at room
   temperature

1 cup plus 2 Tbsp granulated sugar

3 large eggs

1 tsp vanilla extract

1½ Tbsp lightly packed grated
   lemon zest (about 1½ medium),
   preferably organic

SWEET TART LEMON
CANDIED GINGER FROSTING

½ cup unsalted butter, at room
   temperature

1 cup confectioners' (icing) sugar

½ cup lemon curd

3 Tbsp minced candied ginger

LEMON FAIRY CAKES *with* SWEET TART LEMON CANDIED GINGER FROSTING

If you love lemon, I guarantee you will love these cupcakes. My brother Luke calls them Arnold Palmer cupcakes after the famous drink of half lemonade, half iced tea.

The icing is like a frosting version of those amazing little lemon candies. It's light, creamy, fluffy and a pale buttery yellow. I recommend making your own lemon curd if you have the time. It really doesn't take long and makes such a difference to the icing. If you use a storebought lemon curd, add a little lemon juice, as it is usually way too sweet. The icing can be kept in the fridge, tightly covered, for up to four days. Before using, allow it to come to room temperature and give it a good beat with an electric mixer to get it back to its original fluffy texture.

Preheat the oven to 350°F.

Line twelve ½-cup muffin cups with paper cupcake liners.

Place the milk and tea bags in a heavy saucepan and bring to a boil, being careful not to let it boil over. Remove the pan from the heat and allow the tea bags to further infuse the milk for 10 minutes while it cools. Remove the tea bags.

Sift together the cake flour and baking powder in a bowl.

Using an electric mixer, beat the butter and granulated sugar in a large bowl for 4 minutes.

Add the eggs and the vanilla and beat on high for another 2 minutes, or until the batter is pale yellow and fluffy. Scrape down the sides of the bowl with a spatula.

On low speed, beat in the flour mixture in 3 additions, alternating with 2 additions of the steeped milk, scraping down the sides of the bowl between additions. Gently fold in the lemon zest.

Fill each muffin cup with ⅓ cup batter, or until it is just below the top of the paper cup.

Bake the cupcakes for 20 to 25 minutes, or until a cake tester inserted into the middle comes out clean. Remove the cupcakes from the pan and cool completely on a wire rack.

For the frosting, combine the butter and confectioners' sugar in a bowl and beat with an electric mixer on high for 2 minutes, or until light and fluffy. Beat in the lemon curd and ginger on medium to incorporate. Cover and refrigerate the icing for 20 minutes. Before using, beat the frosting on high for 1 minute, or until the texture is light and fluffy.

Ice the cupcakes with the frosting.

LEMON CURD

Store this homemade lemon curd in the refrigerator for up to a week. It's also great spread on Mom's crêpes (page 16).

Combine ½ cup unsalted butter, at room temperature, and 1 cup granulated sugar in a bowl. Beat with an electric mixer on high for 2 minutes.

Add 2 large eggs and 2 large egg yolks and beat for 1 minute. Add ⅔ cup freshly squeezed lemon juice and beat for 20 seconds. (Don't be alarmed at the curdled appearance. The mixture will smooth out when it is cooked.)

Transfer the mixture to a heavy saucepan. Cook over low heat, stirring constantly, for 2 to 3 minutes, or until smooth. Increase the heat to medium and cook, stirring, for 4 to 5 minutes, or until the mixture thickens to the consistency of light custard. Do not let it boil.

Remove from the heat and stir in 1 Tbsp lightly packed grated lemon zest. Transfer the mixture to a bowl and press a piece of plastic wrap onto the surface to prevent a skin from forming. Refrigerate.

Makes about 1½ cups.

Linda

RED BERRY CLAFOUTI

2 generous cups fresh raspberries

1 generous cup roughly chopped fresh
 strawberries (about 7 oz/200 g)

4 large eggs

7 Tbsp granulated sugar

1 vanilla bean, or 2 tsp vanilla extract

1⅓ cups almond flour

1 cup 35% (whipping) cream

1 cup crème fraîche (page 201)

1 Tbsp raspberry liqueur
 (e.g., Chambord), Lillet
 or Pineau des Charentes (page 192),
 or orange juice

In Provence, clafouti is made with dark red cherries and a pan-cake-like batter. My clafouti has evolved from a recipe given to me by a French chef who added almond flour and used berries instead of cherries. I in turn put in some crème fraîche and a touch of liqueur. The berries rest in a batter that falls somewhere between pudding and cake.

Preheat the oven to 350°F.

Spread the raspberries and strawberries evenly over the bottom of an 8-cup shallow baking dish.

Whisk the eggs in a large bowl until frothy. Add the sugar and whisk until fully mixed. Cut the vanilla bean lengthwise and scrape the seeds into the eggs, mixing in completely.

Stir in the almond flour, cream, crème fraîche and liqueur. Pour the batter over the berries.

Place the baking dish in a larger roasting pan and pour warm water into the roasting pan until it comes halfway up the sides of the baking dish. Bake on the middle rack of the oven for 25 to 30 minutes, or until the batter is just set. Serve while just warm.

. . . .

KITCHEN HINT

ALMOND FLOUR

Almond flour, sometimes called almond meal or ground almonds, can be found in most gourmet and health food stores. If you wish to make your own, in a food processor, grind 1 cup slivered almonds with 1 Tbsp of the sugar called for in the recipe until the nuts have a very fine consistency. Freeze if you are not using it right away.

Makes about 1¼ cups.

. . . .

Devin

MILE-HIGH ZEBRA CAKE *with* FLUFFY VANILLA CREAM CHEESE FROSTING
(photo page 214)

My nine-year-old niece, Sierra, is a chocolate nut. Until she was six, it was a miracle if we could get her to eat anything other than bread and chocolate cake. I made this cake with her in mind.

It is the best chocolate cake I have ever come across. For those of you who secretly love the light airiness of those boxed cake mixes, this is the homemade version you have been looking for. For a special occasion, I like to decorate the top with a pile of fresh strawberries and raspberries.

The frosting can be made a day ahead and stored in an airtight container in the fridge. Bring it to room temperature and beat on high for a minute before using.

Preheat the oven to 350°F.

Butter three 9-inch round cake pans. Place a round of parchment paper in the bottom of each pan and butter again.

For the cake, sift together the flour, cocoa, baking soda, baking powder and salt in a large bowl. Add the sugar and whisk together.

In a separate bowl, beat together the eggs, buttermilk, warm water and oil with a mixer on low until combined.

Add the wet ingredients to the dry ingredients and mix on low for 3 minutes. Scrape down the sides of the bowl partway through mixing. Divide the batter evenly among the cake pans.

Bake the cakes for about 35 minutes, or until a cake tester comes out clean. If you cannot fit all the pans on the same oven rack, rotate the pans halfway through baking.

Let the cakes cool in the pans for 15 minutes. Run a knife

CAKE

2½ cups unbleached all-purpose flour

1¼ cups Dutch process cocoa powder

2½ tsp baking soda

1¼ tsp baking powder

1 tsp kosher salt

2½ cups granulated sugar

3 large eggs

1¼ cups buttermilk

1¼ cups warm water

⅔ cup vegetable oil

VANILLA CREAM CHEESE FROSTING

8 oz (250 g) cream cheese, at room temperature

1 cup unsalted butter, at room temperature

Pinch of kosher salt

Seeds of ½ vanilla bean, or 1 tsp vanilla extract

2¼ cups confectioners' (icing) sugar, sifted

around the edge of the pans and remove the cakes to cool completely on a wire rack.

For the frosting, combine the cream cheese, butter, salt and vanilla seeds in a large bowl. Beat with an electric mixer on high for about 3 minutes, or until light and creamy.

Add the confectioners' sugar in two batches (so as not to make a mess of your kitchen with flying white powder). Beat for 2 minutes to aerate.

Once the cakes are completely cool, cut off the slightly domed center of the cakes with a serrated knife to make the tops completely level. Frost the cakes with a thick layer of frosting between each layer. (Don't frost the outside of the cake, just between the layers and the top. The icing will softly ooze from between the layers of the cake, creating alternating black and white layers.)

NANA'S ZEBRA CAKE

My grandmother made a much simpler version of zebra cake. She would buy chocolate wafer cookies and sandwich them with whipped cream in a long train. Then she covered the whole thing with a layer of whipped cream, wrapped the cake in foil and stuck it in the refrigerator overnight. The next day, when the cookies were soft and tender, she would cut thick slices on the diagonal. Later we learned she'd got the recipe off the back of the cookie package, but who cares? I used to make this with my niece; it's a great (but messy) cooking project for kids.

KITCHEN HINT

COCOA

Most cocoas are labeled Dutch process or natural. Dutch process cocoa is made with beans that have been treated with an alkaline substance to reduce their acidity. This results in a smoother, richer chocolate taste and darker color when used in baking.

ACKNOWLEDGMENTS

Martin Connell, husband, father and official taster, who bumped up his exercise routine while we were testing recipes. Luke Connell, son, brother and part-time recipe tester, whose advice was always stellar.

Family members Seanna, Ted, Sierra, John, Shauna, Pyper, Finn, Lindsey, Jim, Phil, Hope, Calla, Adrien, Josie and John — all great sports through months of menu tasting and photo shoots.

Emily Gondosch, researcher and fact-finder extraordinaire, and Darcy Morris, who enthusiastically ate all our experiments — successes and failures.

Doug Pepper, McClelland and Stewart publisher, who believed in this book from the very first moment, and talented designer Terri Nimmo, for making our visual concepts a reality.

Shelley Tanaka, our spectacular editor and detail-oriented guide to what makes a professional manuscript.

Doug Bradshaw, our favorite photographer, and gifted food stylist Claire Stubbs, who once again hit a home run.

Adrien Blanchat for helping to show our best side.

Jan Sherk, recipe tester and food stylist for our location shots.

Illustrator Courtney Wotherspoon, who left her drawing board to co-ordinate our location shoot.

The ACE Bakery team of Rosalind Whelan, Marcus Mariathas and Phil Gaudet, who have always supported us.

Suzanne Fitzgerald, who kept us organized through months of recipe testing, developing and writing.

Hyacinth and Annette for keeping our workspace tidy and clean, and loving everything we cooked.

Louise Dennys, whose invaluable advice and support were unwavering from concept to completion, and Ric Young, who was cheeky enough to suggest our title.

Patachou, The Cookbook Store, L'Atelier, The Cat's Meow, Harvest Wagon, French Country, Caffe Doria, Kay & Young Flowers — all great Toronto shops that were kind enough to allow us to photograph on their premises.

INDEX

LINDA HAYNES

Linda studied journalism and worked on air in television before switching to a career as a television and advertising producer. In 1983 she and her husband, Martin Connell, started Calmeadow, a non-profit organization that provided small loans to low-income micro-entrepreneurs. She is the co-founder of ACE Bakery, an artisan bakery that sells bread in Canada, the United States and the Bahamas.

Linda has written two best-selling cookbooks—*The ACE Bakery Cookbook* and *More from ACE Bakery*—and her recipes have appeared in numerous newspapers and magazines. She has been honored with the International Association of Culinary Professionals (IACP) Award for Philanthropy, the CESO Award for International Development, the Entrepreneur of the Year Ernst & Young, and was chosen as one of the Canadian Women Who Make a Difference. In 2006, she was awarded the Order of Canada in the field of philanthropy.

Linda and her husband share five children and four grandchildren. They are based in Toronto.

DEVIN CONNELL

Devin attended high school at The Bishop Strachan School in Toronto and graduated in graphic design from Parson's New School of Design in New York. She has studied art at Sothebys in London. In Paris she took art history classes at the American University as well as attending classes at the Cordon Bleu.

Devin has been a graphic designer at Roots Canada for the babies' wear line and worked with the creative director of Selfridges in London, England. After spending time in the kitchens of The Slanted Door restaurant organization in San Francisco, she is now the owner of Delica Kitchen, a wholesome, fresh and all-natural sandwich, salad and soup bar in Toronto.